"We need a lot more books on integrating faith and work, but not all teaching on this subject is of equal value. In particular, I've noticed over the years that a lot of such books tend to be intellectualistic, all about 'applying biblical principles' in a way that leaves out the changed heart that we need to glorify God in our work. That changed heart, with its reordered loves, comes from an application of the gospel of grace. Bryan Chapell as always is an expert on this subject. I'm grateful for this important contribution to the faith-and-work Christian movement."

Tim Keller, Pastor Emeritus, Redeemer Church

"All too often, we think of God's calling solely in terms of responding to a divine summons to pastoral ministry or missions. But in *Grace at Work*, Bryan Chapell does a masterful job of helping us understand the dignity and grace involved in serving in any role to which God has led and gifted us. The biblical concept of vocation is one that every believer should understand, as it opens the door to faithfulness and kingdom service in any job or profession. In this book, Chapell aids us in that understanding and helps us see how we can be part of God's great mission no matter what our work."

Michael Duduit, Editor, *Preaching* magazine; Dean of Clamp Divinity School, Anderson University

"Bryan Chapell handles a neglected subject, our daily work, with the lucid writing and pastoral heart we have all come to expect from him. I found my own discipling of others received a needed correction; it's easy for ministry leaders to focus so much on our work on Sundays that we neglect our people's work the rest of the week. Dr. Chapell rightly dignifies all work, out of the clear teaching of Scripture, yet also gently brings the gospel to bear on our failings in our work. I will be using this book to help the men and women under my care receive the encouragement and honor that they deserve as they get up on yet another Monday morning."

Dane Ortlund, Senior Pastor, Naperville Presbyterian Church; author, *Gentle and Lowly* and *Deeper*

"I have known Bryan Chapell for over thirty years. I can count on one hand the people I know who exemplify wisdom, brilliance, trust, humility, leadership, and counsel, and Bryan is on that list. I'm honored to be his friend and endorse the vital lessons he teaches to countless others through his books and podcasts. Buckle your seatbelt as his ideas will challenge you as they have me, both in business and all walks of life."

Benjamin F. (Tad) Edwards IV, Chairman and CEO Benjamin F. Edwards & Co.

"For anyone in the workplace looking for encouragement in these challenging times, I would highly recommend *Grace at Work*. A better understanding of God's grace in us and through us in everyday life and work is clearly presented."

AJ Rassi, retired officer, Caterpillar Inc.

"With characteristic clarity and honesty, Bryan Chapell has written a realistic, biblical, grace-driven guide to Christians who seek to be faithful and fruitful in their work. Punctuated with lively illustrations, this book nurtures the disciples' hope of loving God and neighbor at work."

Dan Doriani, Professor of Biblical and Systematic Theology, Covenant Seminary; Founder and Director, Center for Faith & Work St. Louis

"As a part of the 1 percent of the church who, according to Ephesians 2:14, is tasked to equip the 99 percent of you who are called to do your ministry in the workplace, I'm so excited for this book. There is indeed dignity, purpose, and grace as you exercise your God-given gifts for his glory in your occupation. God calls you to minister in your workplaces in ways that church ministers never could. Receive this high calling with heavenly joy! Play your indispensable part in the great commission!"

Michael Oh, CEO, Lausanne Movement

"*Grace at Work* is a gift to Christians needing Jesus's assurance that their work matters. God has woven together Bryan Chapell's work experience as a common laborer and hourly employee, his pastoral experience with farmers and CEOs, and his communication experience as a journalist and homiletics professor to produce an encouraging read for pastor and layman alike. This is a real masterpiece for the church!"

George Robertson, Senior Pastor, Second Presbyterian Church, Memphis, Tennessee

"Whether you are a preacher or a teacher, or whether you work with your hands or sit at a screen each day, your job matters. As a believer in Jesus, you have a vocation, a calling that can bring glory to God and good for others. In *Grace at Work*, my friend Bryan Chapell gives practical and encouraging wisdom to believers regarding our work—no matter our location or vocation."

Ed Stetzer, Executive Director, Billy Graham Center for Evangelism, Wheaton College

Grace at Work

Other Crossway Books by Bryan Chapell

Holiness by Grace: Delighting in the Joy That Is Our Strength (2011)

Unlimited Grace: The Heart Chemistry That Frees from Sin and Fuels the Christian Life (2016)

Using Illustrations to Preach with Power (2001)

Grace at Work

Redeeming the Grind and the Glory of Your Job

Bryan Chapell

WHEATON, ILLINOIS

Library of Congress Cataloging-in-Publication Data

Names: Chapell, Bryan, author.

Title: Grace at work : redeeming the grind and the glory of your job / Bryan Chapell.

Description: Wheaton, Illinois : Crossway, 2022. | Includes bibliographical references and index.

Identifiers: LCCN 2021056713 (print) | LCCN 2021056714 (ebook) | ISBN 9781433578236 (trade paperback) | ISBN 9781433578243 (pdf) | ISBN 9781433578250 (mobipocket) | ISBN 9781433578267 (epub)

Subjects: LCSH: Work—Religious aspects—Christianity. | Vocation—Christianity. | Grace (Theology)

Classification: LCC BT738.5 .C43 2022 (print) | LCC BT738.5 (ebook) | DDC 248.8/8—dc23/eng/20220128

LC record available at https://lccn.loc.gov/2021056713

LC ebook record available at https://lccn.loc.gov/2021056714

Crossway is a publishing ministry of Good News Publishers.

BP   31   30   29   28   27   26   25   24   23   22
15   14   13   12   11   10   9   8   7   6   5   4   3   2   1

To the dear people of Grace Presbyterian Church in Peoria, Illinois

*These messages were first delivered to you, as you sought
the will of God for the work of your lives from the truth of
his word. Your love for the Lord and this pastor has made
this book possible. I echo the words of the apostle to express
how blessed were Kathy's and my years among you:*

*"I thank my God in all my remembrance of you, always in every
prayer of mine for you all making my prayer with joy, because of your
partnership in the gospel from the first day until now." (Phil. 1:3–5)*

Contents

Introduction

MOST CHRISTIANS SPEND their working lives hoping that God will find some way to use their efforts for his priorities. They may not be able to see how God can use what they consider their daily grind or, by contrast, the glorious pursuits for which they are passionate. Still, because they are God's people, they pray that he will provide some real connection between their work and his mission for our world.

Isn't that what we all pray? We pray for the connection because we question, Is there any purpose in my work beyond a paycheck? Is there some mission for me beyond making money? Am I responsible before God only to put in the hours to fill up my bank account, pay the mortgage, feed my family, and not feel guilty about the size of the check in the offering plate? Isn't there some greater purpose for me that would give my life's efforts dignity beyond how I appear to others or think about myself?

These are common and persistent questions that weigh on sincere Christians until they recognize that God's people are being called to his mission not just in Sunday worship but in the everyday workplace. A key aspect of God's everyday grace is his giving us the means and opportunity to show his character, demonstrate his care, and fulfill his purposes.

God calls us to use the work skills, talents, and resources that he provides for extending the influence of the kingdom of God into every dimension of our lives and world. Understanding this calling enables us to see that our jobs have a dignity we may never have previously understood.

A few years ago, I was speaking at a career conference for Christian college students. Because my background and training are in journalism, the topic of my talk was the calling of Christian journalism. I tried to explain to the students how Christian journalists can have a powerful influence on their culture not only by writing articles on Christian subjects but also by bringing a Christian perspective to their descriptions of human relationships and world events.

After my talk, a young woman came up to me and said, "Your talk just made me feel guilty, because the kind of journalism I want to do is to write articles for fashion magazines. I have a love for fashion, but I know it's vacuous and vain and doesn't honor God at all."

"Listen," I said, "if you think what you're going to be doing for a career is vacuous and vain, please do not give your life to that work. But if you are able to express the creativity and beauty of God as a fashion writer, you could be a wonderful Christian influence on an industry that needs to talk about beauty without vulgarity."

Our sense of our life's purpose changes dramatically when we begin to recognize that all kinds of work possess qualities of divine mission—not just the jobs of preachers or missionaries, and not just those of CEOs and brain surgeons.

God is calling the cop and the carpenter and the concrete layer to experience the dignity of their work as he uses their jobs to help others, improve lives, and spread the influence of his kingdom in the world. In the skills we express, in the products we make, in the way we work, in the impact of our labors on society and on the relationships affected by our work, we are instruments of God's redeeming work in a broken world. God intends to demonstrate his grace through us.

We need to claim this truth so that we don't belittle or disparage our own vocation with, "I'm just a tentmaker." What? You mean like Paul? "Just a fisherman." What? You mean like Peter? "Just a carpenter." What? You mean like Jesus? In every vocation, we have the ability to take the image of God into the work that we do and, in doing so, help people understand the goodness of who God is, the care that he has for us, and the diverse professions he has created for the care of his world and its people.

This book is designed to help us understand and more fully experience personal dignity and divine purpose in the varied jobs that we do to serve God and all that he loves. No matter how isolated our Monday work may seem from our Sunday worship, God is yet providing his grace for the glory and the grind of our jobs.

When we realize that every honest job exists on the holy ground of God's calling, then we will rejoice in the mission we have at work. Such joy invigorates us for every task, whether menial or majestic, with the understanding that each can bring glory to the one who sent his Son to serve us.

Ultimately, we do not serve a company or a boss or even our family's needs, but our Lord, who smiles upon our labors, values our sweat, and dries our tears with the grace of knowing he will use every effort that honors him. Even when we have not considered or advanced his honor, his work is not done. Instead, he offers pardon and the grace to try again with the assurance that our labors for him are not in vain.

The new contract without hidden clauses, the lunchtime conversation kept clean, the cleanup job that cuts no corners, the expense report that is true, the hate speech not entered, the rage not expressed, the architecture kept beautiful, the benefits plan made fair, the government policy that is just, the discipline procedure that is merciful—all bring glory to the one who shows his character and care through his people.

All such work done and evil shunned come from the heart of a God who has shown us his grace in his word so that we can know and show his grace at work.

1

Dignity

AUTHOR STEVE GARBER writes that most Christian people "spend their lives in the marketplaces of the world, hoping as they do that there is some honest connection between what they do and the work of God in the world. They yearn to see their vocations as integral, not incidental, to the *missio Dei* [the mission of God]."

Isn't that what we all want to know at times? Does God have a mission for my work? Does God have any purpose for what I do? Am I just putting in the hours to fill up the bank account? Or is there some greater purpose in my work? Can I fulfill God's mission at work?

Garber goes on to say, "Sorrowfully, most of the time the church teaches the opposite . . . that our vocations are incidental, on the sidelines of what God really cares about."[1] We assume that the spiritual priorities concentrated in preaching, witnessing, missionary endeavors, and worship activities are God's main concern. So everything else is secondary or meant to serve these "really godly" purposes.

I recognize that there is the tendency among pastors, myself included, to see what is said in the Scriptures as applying primarily to the life of the church and not thinking carefully about what people are called to do the rest of the week. I need to remember over and over again that Sunday is for Monday, and that we are being called by God to do his work not just in worship but in the workplace.

An old word that may help us is *vocation*.

In our culture, we often use the word *vocation* virtually the same way that we use the word *occupation*. But it's really quite different in the history of the church. Our vocation is our calling. The word *vocation* actually means "calling" and originates in what God has called us to do to fulfill his mission in our lives. That's a different focus from our occupation, which is how we earn a living to fulfill our needs and desires.

As Christians we need to understand that our occupation actually has a vocation in it and that we are called to use our gifts and talents and resources for the extending of the kingdom of God. Only then will we begin to see that our jobs have a dignity we may never have understood. God intends to show aspects of his goodness and glory to others by the work we do during the week, as well as by the worship we offer on Sunday.

Garber challenges me when he continues writing, "When was the last time that architects and builders, teachers and librarians, doctors and nurses, artists and journalists, lawyers and judges were prayed for in your congregation? We need to keep praying for the Young Life staff people and for the Wycliffe Bible Translators, but we also need to pray for the butchers and the bakers, and the candlestick makers, too."[2] I would add that we need not only to pray for them but to equip them for their mission in all walks of life and corners of the world, wherever God calls them to display his purposes and priorities.

The Dignity of Work

Your work is your mission field, and because of that, there is a God-given dignity in what you do. How do I know that there is dignity in your work? Because that dignity is first revealed to us in Genesis 2:15: "The Lord God took the man and put him in the garden of Eden to work it and keep it."

When we "work" something, we make it flourish. And when we "keep" it, we sustain it. We don't waste it or abuse it. The Lord told Adam in his first job description, "I'm calling you to production and to conservation." In other words, we are colaborers with God in his creation care. Production and conservation are part of what we are called to do in God's world. That's our job description. That's our labor. That's our mission too.

Good farming methods, pollution control, mining and land management, energy production and conservation—all modern concerns—are actually being addressed in these early pages of Genesis, where we are called to consider not only how to produce what we need but also to conserve so that God's world itself is honored.

Label before Labor

One of the important observations in the first chapter of Genesis is that we get our label before we get our labor. In other words, before we are told what to do, we are told *who we are* in God's eyes. Genesis 1:26–27 says the following:

Then God said, "Let us make man in our image, after our likeness. And let them have dominion over the fish of the sea and over the birds of the heavens and over the livestock and over all the earth and over every creeping thing that creeps on the earth." So God created man in his own image, in the image of God he created him; male and female he created them.

To be created in the image of God is to reflect his character and care, to be one who mirrors him. And here we are being told that even though our genders may vary, God's fundamental intent for men and women does not vary: both have the responsibility before God of reflecting him in the world.

Of course, being God's image and mirror doesn't mean that we are God. When we talk about young people being the spitting image of their father, we're not saying that they are the same as their father but that, when you see them, you're reminded of their father. In the same way, when people observe our work in the world, they should be reminded of our Father, especially his character and care.

When the Bible says we have been created "in the image of God," it is astonishing to realize that this label is given to no other aspect of God's creation.

Reflect on that for a moment.

Think of the most amazing sunset you've ever seen, the grandeur of the oceans, and the majesty of the mountains. Think of the beautiful images from the Hubble telescope of exploding galaxies and of our own glorious Milky Way, and yet not one of those grand creations is identified as bearing the image of God.

As image bearers, we are actually given a dignity above everything in the universe. That is what the psalmist says in Psalm 8:3–5:

> When I look at your heavens, the work of your fingers,
>> the moon and the stars, which you have set in place,
> what is man that you are mindful of him,
>> and the son of man that you care for him?
>
> Yet you have made him a little lower than the heavenly
>> beings
> and crowned him with glory and honor.

We are "fearfully and wonderfully made." I know it may sound a little boastful, but we are awesome! We need to realize what God is saying to us: "You have the special privilege of being my image bearers in every place that you're called, including your work."

Our Value Is Not Based on What We Do

Genesis tells us that people were created in God's image before he assigned them the task of working and keeping the garden. Why is this important? It is important because God is saying, "I'm not determining whether you're an image bearer based upon what you accomplish." The reason we value the unborn and the infirm is that they are still image bearers of God, regardless of what they do. What they have done or can do is not the basis of their value.

This notion that we get our label before we are assigned our labor is one of the Bible's earliest explanations of the gospel. When you truly grasp the profound beauty of being valued by God before you have done work for God—treasured for who you are, not for what you have accomplished—then your life will never be the same. You begin to live in the freedom and power of knowing that God is for you not because of what you provide for him, but because of what he provides for you. God's love and mercy are never based upon what you do but on his grace toward you.

God has been signaling that message from the beginning of the Bible so that our hearts are made ready to receive his grace and eager to reflect his glory. The care of God that culminates in the provision of Jesus Christ for those who could not earn or deserve his mercy radiates from the simple truth that we are given a loving label before we are assigned our life's labor.

Because you are an image bearer, you have value and dignity before you're ever given a job assignment. And whether you become the president of a large corporation or serve God as a custodian in a public school, your value and worth before God never change, since each career path is pursued by a divine image bearer with equal dignity in the Lord's eyes.

How We Treat Ourselves and Others

Being created in God's image has many applications for how we view ourselves. Self-hatred is ruled out. All the rejection we fear because of our sin, our backgrounds, our lack of performance, and our body image not being what we think it should be—these should also be ruled out. God is saying to us, "I want you to remember that you're the spitting image of me." As a result, I get to treat myself as one who bears the image of my heavenly Father.

The knowledge that all people are created in God's image should impact how we treat others. Our tendency is to treat people the way they treat us. If we believe one of our coworkers has treated us unfairly, we're tempted to retaliate. Or if our supervisor is difficult or demanding, that may affect how our hearts respond to his or her leadership.

But when we realize that people's image bearing is not based on what they do, that is a game changer. We may think that they aren't very good examples of God's image, but their value is not based on what they do but on who they are in God's eyes.

Further, because every person is created in God's image, our goal should be to help them flourish. How can we do that? If you're an employer, look at your employees and ask, "How is their healthcare? Are they receiving appropriate benefits? Are they paid a fair wage for their work?" Those created in God's image deserve our care.

If you're an employee, you should treat your coworkers—even the difficult ones—with dignity and respect, remembering that God's love and grace toward you are not based on your actions. You should also do whatever you can to help the people you work with to flourish rather than focusing solely on your own advancement and success. Those created in God's image deserve our service and sacrifice.

When We Fail to See God's Image in Others

Recently I saw in the news that a bus in the Middle East was forcibly stopped on the road. Terrorists got on the bus and asked people to recite portions of the Quran. If they were not able to do so, they were either abused or murdered. These terrorists were able to justify their actions because they viewed non-Muslims as less than human.

The same thing happened in World War II. The Nazis declared that Jews were subhuman and therefore should be exterminated. If you've ever visited a Holocaust museum or seen images of the Nazi death camps, then you'll realize the atrocities that can occur when we fail to affirm that all people are created in God's image.

The history of the United States also provides grim reminders of what happens when people are viewed as less than human. Although the Declaration of Independence proclaimed that "all men are created equal, that they are endowed by their Creator with certain unalienable Rights, that among these are Life, Liberty, and the pursuit of Happiness," these God-given rights were not extended to Native Americans or African-Americans.

As a result, our nation impoverished "Indians" and viewed their genocide as acceptable. The terrible abuses of slavery were justified because black people were viewed as subhuman property. These abuses continued—and still continue—far beyond the Civil War because people of one race consider themselves superior to another.

One of the greatest blights on contemporary society is the result of a similar conclusion about unborn children. In the 1973 Supreme Court case known as Roe v. Wade, Justice Harry Blackmun spoke for the majority when he wrote "that the word 'person,' as used in the Fourteenth Amendment, does not include the unborn."[3] Since that time, there have been over sixty million abortions in the United States alone.

By contrast, Genesis tells us that every person, regardless of color, nationality, religion, or age, is an image bearer of God. The Psalms and the prophet Jeremiah add that God knows us—person and purpose—even as we are "knit together" in our mother's womb (Ps. 139:13; Jer. 1:5). Therefore, we are obligated to treat people of every nationality, ethnicity, ability, or age with dignity and respect.

Labor Comes before the Fall

We have already seen the dignity of work affirmed in Genesis 2:15, which says, "The LORD God took the man and put him in the garden of Eden to work it and keep it." But that's not the full message of what's happening in Genesis. We also know that our work has dignity because our labor comes before the fall of humanity.

Do you know what I mean when I talk about the fall? According to Genesis 3:15, that's when human sin caused corruption and decay to enter the world, along with all the evil, pain, and difficulty we now experience.

But this fall of humanity described in Genesis 3:15 comes after our job description in Genesis 2:15. Why is that important? It is important because it means that labor is not bad. Labor is not evil. Of course, after the fall labor became more difficult, but it is not a curse—it is a prior gift from God that gives our lives purpose.

Why is it important to affirm the goodness of labor? It is important because you and I sometimes say to ourselves, "If I just didn't have to work, life would be so pleasant." Right?

I can remember when I was in college, and one of the jobs through which I earned my tuition was bussing tables in the student cafeteria. The work was dirty and messy and not much fun. After a semester or two of bussing tables, the food service changed hands. New management came in and said, "We've got a new rule: For one price, every student can eat all the food they want every day." That sounded good until the food company began to realize that students can eat a LOT of food! Supervisors also discovered that students were taking extra food out of the cafeteria to eat over the weekend when the food service was closed. So my bosses decided that someone needed to guard the door. Someone had to do the job of sitting by the exit to watch for people who were stealing food.

Every one of us wanted that job! No more bussing tables, no more cleaning up messes, and no more handling dirty dishes. All you had to do was sit by the door and nothing more.

Doesn't that sound like a great job? I got the job and discovered it was awful. You couldn't do your homework, because you were supposed to be looking for people stealing food. All you could do was watch time pass and students pass by. But very quickly those students learned that if they hid their food in their backpacks, you couldn't know whether they were stealing food.

In the end, my job as a "food policeman" was pointless and boring. The hours crawled by, and I was miserable.

Some of you have that same experience at a different stage of life. You think to yourself, *When I retire, I will play golf all day, every day. It's going to be so wonderful!* As it turns out, it's wonderful for about three weeks.

Then you tell yourself, *I've got to do something! I need to volunteer at the soup kitchen or tutor neighborhood kids. Maybe my spouse and I need to move to where we can help with our grandkids. I need to take a part-time job or be useful in some way.* Why? Because you were made to work, to enable things and people to flourish.

That's how God has designed us.

When we begin to recognize that work is not evil but is actually something that gives our days purpose and our lives a sense of worth, then we begin to view our labor in a very different way. We discover that work is dignifying and doing nothing is dehumanizing. Nothing is more wearying to the soul than no work at all.

Irresponsible Lifestyles

A few years ago, a Texas teen stole beer from a store and went for a drive while intoxicated. He struck and killed four people on the side of the road, and a passenger in his car became paralyzed and suffered brain damage. When the teen went to trial, a psychologist suggested that the young man was suffering from "affluenza," claiming that his affluent upbringing had failed to teach him right from wrong. Prosecutors sought a twenty-year prison sentence, but the judge sentenced him to only ten years of probation.[4]

We may all shake our heads and say, "Well, that's crazy," but we should grieve for any young man who doesn't know right and wrong, or doesn't know how to be productive, or doesn't know how to make his way in the world because he doesn't have any understanding of work or responsibility.

We should also recognize that this story in a different version is spreading across our culture. Do you realize that 30 percent of all men of working age in this culture are not working? There are many reasons for this. Some workers lack the skills needed for all but the lowest-paid jobs. Some jobs have been eliminated because of technology advances or cheaper overseas labor. Some have discovered government benefits that enable them to avoid working:

In a study for the Mercatus Center of George Mason University, Scott Winship reports that "75 percent of inactive prime-age men are in a household that received some form of government transfer payment." Mr. Winship believes that government disability benefits in particular are one reason for the lack of interest in work.[5]

Another trend toward irresponsibility is the growth of the video-gaming culture in our society. Many young men and women are spending countless hours every day or many hours of the night just gaming away. They may lose sleep, college opportunities, and work advancement with addictions to meaningless competitions that consume time and energy but produce nothing.

Do you know what I would call a pastime where I spend all my time, all my money, all my resources, pursuing things that are not real and that never will benefit me or society? I would call it slavery. And those who are enslaved by such meaningless pursuits ultimately lose all respect for themselves.

Work gives us dignity, because work itself is dignified. When we begin to understand God's perspective on work, then we realize that it is actually a form of worship.

Our Labor Follows God's Rest

Genesis 2:2 gives us another important insight into the nature of our work: "On the seventh day God finished his work that he had done, and he rested on the seventh day from all his work that he had done."

On the very first Sabbath day, the Lord had finished all of his work, and therefore he rested—he wasn't tired; he simply came to the end of his creation plan. But when God ceased that work, he wasn't finished with his work in and for us. When God ceased his work, he gave humanity its work of tending his world (Gen. 2:15). In essence, God is saying to us, "I've completed my work of establishing the creation; now it's your turn to work, to make things flourish and to conserve my creation."

In other words, through our own labor, we are continuing God's work in the world. Of course, we know that after the fall of humanity, weeds started to grow and corruption entered the world. For this reason, the work of humanity never stops, and God's intention to bless through our work never ceases.

We are meant to continue to plow under the weeds and to push back the corruption. In this way our job extends the glory and goodness of God made evident by his creation, even against the corruption that's here. This is God's mission for each of us.

There are many ways in which Christians can think about their work honoring God. We work to provide for our families, which is a very good and appropriate means of fulfilling responsibilities God gives us for the care of loved ones.

Another responsibility that can be fulfilled in our work is our witness to unbelievers. Although that, too, is a valid objective, you need to remember that your company did not hire you to be a Christian witness. And if you think that's how you should spend large amounts of your time on your job, that's going to be frustrating to both you and your boss. God requires us to represent him with integrity, giving our energies and resources to the job we were hired to do (Col. 3:23).

An additional reason we work is so that we can be generous to the church and to the mission of God in the world. Our resources can help to fund food banks, homeless shelters, ministries to battered wives, Bible translation and distribution, and those who preach the gospel throughout the world.

All these are appropriate reasons for working. But we will miss the deepest joys and neglect the most profound impact of our vocation if we do not recognize that our work is itself intended to extend the influence of God's kingdom to every corner of creation. Our work is not valuable simply because it provides for some Christian ministries. The work itself is an instrument of God, pushing back the corruption of the fall. God is mowing down the weeds of the world with our work.

The Spread of God's Kingdom

As the various chapters of Genesis unfold, we learn more about the dignity of our work. Think carefully about what has been happening in these early chapters:

- In chapters 1 and 2, the garden of Eden is created for the first couple. As they work the garden and enable it to flourish, their material needs are also met.

- By Genesis 3, fields are being plowed in order to undo the effect of the weeds and eventually to create crops that will provide for the needs of various families.

- By Genesis 4, cities begin to form, and societies begin to function. At that time, artisans, musicians, metal workers, and other trades begin to flourish, adding creativity and beauty to the work they do.

- After the great flood and its aftermath are described in Genesis 6–11, a new beginning for creation unfolds with God's plan to redeem his world and to bless all nations in it through the family and faith of Abraham (Gen. 12–17).

What we see in these opening chapters of Genesis is that the work of humanity is spreading the kingdom of God ever more fully, ever more dramatically, as it moves forward from individuals to families to cities to societies to ultimately a gospel that's meant to encompass the world.

The shalom, the peace of God, that was lost through the corruptions and violence that followed the fall—that shalom is being spread again. The expansion is happening through people who are God's image bearers working responsibly for him in his world.

The Impact of Our Work

My father was a circuit preacher for a string of tiny, one-room churches in the rural South, but he made his living in agribusiness. He was raised on a farm and used his love of agriculture to edit farm journals, to help families make enough money to keep farms that had been in their families for generations, to manage landholdings for large corporations, and to take modern farm methods to nations of the developing world to alleviate starvation.

My father began farm life behind a mule-drawn plow, and he ended his career directing seed and fertilizer operations from satellites. He also preached to souls that were starving for the good news of Jesus, and he provided livelihood and life for hungry people. Along the way, he raised six children, coached Little League teams, led charity drives, directed a regional youth organization, and, in his retirement years, crossed racial boundaries to teach parenting classes in urban schools.

I know that my father believed that he was called to preach. But he believed he was no less called to use his farming skills and family experience to make a difference in the lives of many. Both vocations were God-given, God-honoring, and life-blessing. Both explained the character and care of the God my father worshiped. Both enabled others to flourish and dignified the image of God in my father.

When you begin to recognize that your work can further God's purpose and can be part of the dignity you have in the world, you begin to realize that all kinds of work carry that dignity—not just preachers or presidents, and not just CEOs and surgeons. God is calling the cop and the carpenter and the concrete layer to recognize the dignity of their work and to spread his kingdom in the world.

Our work can have a powerful impact on others. Let me give you one example. As I was working on this book, I came across some statistics from the National Bureau of Economic Research. They reported that in the last third of the twentieth century, the portion of the world living on one dollar a day or less dropped by 80 percent. Over a billion people were lifted from dire poverty by the contribution of men and women with engineering technologies that have turned back the darkness.[6] Thank you, engineers!

So much of what we're able to do in changing our world for good isn't just on the spiritual level. As people are employing their various gifts for God's purposes, the world is being transformed in the many different ways that God intends.

The Dignity of Variety

Genesis 4:19–22 gives us an early description of how society began to develop and diversify:

> Lamech took two wives. The name of the one was Adah, and the name of the other Zillah. Adah bore Jabal; he was the father of those who dwell in tents and have livestock. His brother's name was Jubal; he was the father of all those who play the lyre and pipe. Zillah also bore Tubal-cain; he was the forger of all instruments of bronze and iron.

Here we are in the very early stages of human history, and we find God's people in a great variety of professions. Some are raising livestock. Some are musicians. Others are craftsmen or metalworkers. All these different professions are being established as means by which society will flourish and experience the richness and variety of the Lord's blessings. God uses each vocation to fulfill his purposes, and, as a consequence, each honors him.

We need to hear that message so that we don't look down on our own vocation and say, "I'm just a construction worker or a fisherman or a tax collector or a tentmaker." What? You mean like Jesus and his apostles? You have the ability to take the image of God into the work that you do, and in doing so help people understand the goodness of who God is, the care that he has for us, and the diverse professions he has created for our sake.

We sometimes are hard on ourselves because we think highly of other people's gifts but assume that ours are not worthy. That's why I love the words of 1 Peter 4:10: "As each has received a gift, use it to serve one another, as good stewards of God's varied grace."

There is a lot of gender confusion in our culture right now, and sometimes we increase it by narrowing the definition of what it means to be a man or a woman. For example, we might say to a man who's artistic, "Well, that's not manly." But in the earliest chapters of Genesis we are told that there were men who were artisans.

We might say to a woman who is gifted in salesmanship, "You know, that's not very womanly." The Bible does not agree (see the godly woman described in Proverbs 31:16). The Bible describes men and women working in a variety of professions and for a variety of reasons, and such people are to be honored so long as they do not neglect their biblical obligations.

No matter how difficult or onerous the task, when we are working to fulfill responsibilities God gives us, the Bible helps us to avoid thinking, *I'm just not doing something very important.* My musician wife, Kathy, talks about a time that she was changing a particularly yucky diaper of one of our children, and she said to a friend standing beside her, "These hands have played Mozart." The friend replied, "Maybe these hands are diapering the next Mozart!" Undeniably, what those hands were doing was nurturing an eternal soul. And if you are honoring the gifts God has given you, then you are fulfilling the gracious purpose that he intends for your life.

Capturing the Spirit of Work

One of the most telling books I have read recently was not written so recently, but its truths endure. In the book *Work: The Meaning of Your Life*, Lester DeKoster helps readers to see how everyone's work, from the office to the assembly line, is essential to both society and culture. In order to drive home that point, he writes:

> That chair you are lounging in? Could you have made it for yourself? Well, I suppose so, if we mean just the chair!
>
> Perhaps you did in fact go out to buy the wood, the nails, the glue, the stuffing, the springs—and put it all together. But if by making the chair we mean assembling each part from scratch, that's quite another matter. How do we get, say, the wood? Go and fell a tree? But only after first making the tools for that, and putting together some kind of vehicle to haul the wood, and constructing a mill to do the lumber, and roads to drive on from place to place?
>
> In short, a lifetime or two to make one chair! We are physically unable, it is obvious, to provide ourselves from scratch with the household goods we can now see from wherever you and I are sitting—to say nothing of building and furnishing the whole house.[7]

When we begin to see that there's dignity in every vocation, we realize that every job has a purpose of serving others and bringing glory to God.

The Bible tells us, "The eye cannot say to the hand, 'I have no need of you,' nor again the head to the feet, 'I have no need of you.' On the contrary, the parts of the body that seem to be weaker are indispensable" (1 Cor 12:21–22).

One of the artists that Kathy and I appreciated even before we knew her Christian background is a sculptor named Rosalind

Cook. She writes about her experience as an artist in an article appropriately named "Capturing the Spirit in Bronze."

She began sculpting in the 1970s while she was pregnant. And then three more children followed. And as she became caught up in kids, carpools, peanut butter sandwiches, and all that goes into early motherhood, she drifted away from sculpting.

One day, a visiting missionary was in her home and saw the neglected lumps of sculpting clay and asked what they were about. Rosalind looked at her and began to weep. "I have so much joy in sculpting," she said to the missionary, "but what's the significance of that? My work isn't saving souls. It isn't doing anything for anyone."

The missionary then replied, "Rosalind, you are made in God's image. He is your creator. And when you use the gifts of his image, that gives him pleasure."

In her book, Rosalind writes, "Since the missionary came, I gave myself permission to use the gifts God had given me to be the person he meant me to be. So many people live with regrets, because they don't give themselves permission to use the gifts and opportunities God puts into our lives. When we use those gifts, nurture them, grow them, share them, then we have lived life well."[8]

When we are using the gifts that God has given us in the professions to which he has called us, that gives him pleasure even as it gives us purpose—purpose that is plentiful in variety:

Some of you make money with amazing skill and success.

Some of you paint beautifully.

Some of you make incredible music.

Some of you are engineers working on astounding projects.

Some of you are doctors who restore people's health.

Some of you are tradesmen who enable construction, transportation, and communication without which our society cannot function.

Some of you are gifted salespeople who know that until someone sells something, no employer can employ anyone and no employee can provide for any loved one.

Some of you are teachers who help children learn and find the path to their own dignity and purpose.

When we consider the diversity of tasks and talents God gives to his people, we should be awed by the variety and vastness of his care. *We serve a great God who has given so many people so many dignified things to do!* Our work leads us to worship when we understand the grace it is and the goodness it bestows.

That's the message—our work is a channel of God's grace. By work we both receive and dispense the blessings of our Lord.

When we use God's gifts in the calling he gives us, we fulfill his purposes. The tasks may be magnificent or mundane according to the world's accounting or our own estimation, but faithful labor cannot fail to share the goodness and glory of God. So, there is always dignity in our work as we fulfill God's mission for our lives.

2

Purpose

THE OFT-REPEATED STORY is that Martin Luther once asked a bricklayer, "What are you doing?" And the bricklayer replied, "I'm laying bricks." Luther then asked the worker beside him, "What are you doing?" And that bricklayer said, "I'm building a cathedral to the glory of God." That response helped Luther to grasp the reality that every person serves in a holy calling with a holy purpose. In fact, he even said, "We ought to have ordination services for bricklayers."

Because Christ is Lord of all, the work you do for him is holy before God. Abraham Kuyper, who was prime minister of the Netherlands and an influential theologian, once wrote: "There is not a square inch in the whole domain of our human existence over which Christ, who is Sovereign over *all*, does not cry: 'Mine!'"[1]

My goal in this chapter is to enable that reality to penetrate your heart and mind so that you can experience the joy and privilege of serving Christ's purposes wherever he calls you.

I want you to see that the work you do can honor God and bring glory to him.

In the third chapter of Colossians, the apostle Paul writes: "Whatever you do, in word or deed, do everything in the name of the Lord Jesus, giving thanks to God the Father through him" (v. 17). And just so we know that "everything" includes our workplaces, Paul says in verse 23, "Whatever you do, work heartily, as for the Lord and not for men." These verses remind us that in every place we go, we are on holy ground, being called to serve God's purposes.

Our Work and Our Profession

How do we begin to see and act as though the work we do is included in the purposes of Jesus Christ? We begin by understanding that our vocation is truly our *profession*. In our work, we profess what we understand about the nature of our relationship with God and his relationship with us.

What are we actually professing in our work? Colossians 3:17 tells us: "Whatever you do, in word or deed, do everything in the name of the Lord Jesus." If you do something in Jesus's name, you represent him, and you promote him. Everything you do should be in the name of Christ. What that means in the workplace is that we should work as though we have the name of Christ upon us.

I have a friend who's a marathon runner, and he was in a race a few years ago that he knew would be tough, particularly at the end. And knowing what happens at the ends of races, how people call out encouragement, he didn't put his own name on his racing bib but actually wrote the word *Christian*. He knew that when he got to that final mile, and all the people were cheering, they wouldn't call out his name but would say, "Go get 'em, Christian!" "You can do it, Christian!" "Hang in there, Christian!" He ran to represent the name of Christ that he bore.

Reflecting Christ in Our Practices

When we are in the workplace, we bear the name of our Savior. And that has certain implications for every "Christian." We recognize that we are representing his character and his care in our relationships.

Christ's righteousness is to be seen in our practices. So our annual reports and reviews are honest. We don't take advantage of customers in pricing or in billing. Because we represent Christ, we don't cheat the boss on our timecards or on expense reports, even if others do. We don't lie to regulators. We don't lie to the IRS. Why? Because our Lord has written his name on us so that others can see him.

We represent Jesus in all we do. His character and righteousness are represented in our integrity. His justice is to be seen in our fairness. We don't show favoritism, and we don't ride the people we don't like because we are representing Jesus's love for all. We give others the benefit of the doubt and try to treat them as we would like to be treated because that's how Jesus treats us.

Dick Halverson, the longtime pastor of Fourth Presbyterian church in Washington, DC, and at one time the Senate chaplain, spoke of a businessman who'd been converted in his church. The man wanted to make a difference in his workplace and reported to his pastor, "I have decided to give New Testaments to all of my employees and to all of my customers." And Dick Halverson, who knew something of the man, replied, "Well, that's wonderful, but it might be better if you gave them some *respect*."

We bear the name of Jesus in how we treat people with dignity and mercy. We represent his character in such a way that his heart is seen in our compassion. So we give people second chances and opportunity to change. We provide help or coaching for those who are struggling. And we wrestle and weep over the hard decisions when we have to make them.

We are not calloused to people's struggles. We represent the heart of our Savior. We are generous with God's provisions, because we recognize that God's people—and those not yet God's people—need to know him through the ministries of the church and the work of missions.

Finally, to represent his character, his humility is to be seen in our humility. We don't always have to have the first word. We don't always have to have the last word. And we don't have to have the credit.

Those of you who know a little bit about basketball may recall the most famous lesson that coach Dean Smith taught players at the University of North Carolina at Chapel Hill. He told them, "If you make a basket, you always point at the man who passed you the ball." Strutting and showboating were not to be a part of that program. His players knew that they didn't claim the credit; they gave the credit away.

Giving credit away in the workplace can be difficult for Christians because we recognize that even when we are reflecting Christ's character, there can be advantages for us. After all, if your hard work and perseverance are a positive example to others in the office and on business trips, then you may be thought of as the kind of person who should get greater rewards or responsibilities. These are not bad things in themselves and can be aspects of God's blessing upon our faithfulness.

Still, when there are opportunities to speak for the Savior, we should give the credit to him. We use our successes to point to his provision or to the people he has supplied. This is not mere posturing but recognition that all we are and do is a result of God's provision. He enables our successes, and when we mess up, needing his forgiveness and aid, he provides abundantly from his grace what we most need to fulfill his purposes.

Christ should get the credit for what we do and who we are because apart from him we can do nothing (John 15:5). So, we seek to bring a godly example and ethics to our work primarily so that people can know our Savior, not so that they will think highly of us. Ordinarily, living for God brings earthly as well as eternal blessing, but even if godliness requires sacrifice, we offer it so that others can know him. This means, of course, that if we are to reflect Christ, then his character should be evident in practices that honor him even if they cost us.

Reflecting Christ in Our Products

Christ's care should also be reflected in our products. We are, in essence, saying about the things we produce, whether we are on the assembly line or are the company owner, "I stamp the name of Jesus on this product." As Christians, our mission is to put Christ's name on everything we make.

This happens in lots of ways, sometimes even instinctively, if we are believers. When my son Jordan was learning the stock-trading business he was assigned the task of following up on various leads by making endless phone calls. That was dreary, deadening work. You know, one phone call after another phone call after another phone call.

Jordan told us that he was making his phone calls late one evening, and he was very tired. He began speaking to a potential client's voicemail almost on autopilot, reciting the script he had repeated so often. When he finally got to the end of the message, his exhaustion threw him into an instinctive gear generated from years of faith. He concluded the sales call, "And so that's our deal. In Jesus's name. Amen."

After Jordan hung up the phone, he realized that in his weariness he had recited a prayer ending that he wasn't supposed to say to potential commodity clients. He didn't quite know what to do next. So he called the person back and left an apologetic voicemail.

When I heard the story, I laughed but was actually very proud of my son because I knew that his weary words of faith had come from somewhere deep within him. Even in his mundane and repetitive task, he had not left his faith to do his job. In fact, he had instinctively taken Jesus with him on the job—which is not always easy.

Kathy and I lived a long time in St. Louis, where some of the major industries are chemical companies. While we were there, we discovered how people's perceptions of those chemical companies can change over time. Some of the companies produced pesticides that enabled farmers to grow food in the developing nations so they can feed millions of their people. Initially people cheered those companies. Then a decade or two later, people began to say, "You're not feeding millions of people; you're poisoning our world!" I mention this not to make a judgment about any particular company but to remind those who bear the name of Christ that it is always important to examine our jobs and ask, "Is what we are doing truly honoring to God?"

Each Christian should be willing to ask, "Can I stamp Christ's name on this product? Can I take Jesus with me on this job?" Answering may require not only honest evaluation of a product's impact but also a willingness to reevaluate in the light of changing circumstances.

A Christian's determination of the appropriateness of what our work produces or requires should not simply be left to cultural whims or popular opinion. Instead, Christians are obligated to ask God whether our work and our products glorify him according to his word. With an integrated economy that often combines the labors, products, and practices of companies and countries with widely varying standards of ethics and justice, these can be complex questions, but the name we bear requires that we consider them.

The Significance of Our Work

Sometimes the righteousness of what we're producing is not our real struggle. It's the *significance* of what we're producing.

Not long ago, I was in Oregon at a pastors' conference, and during a break, the hosts took us to a cheese factory, one of the largest cheese producers in the United States. The tour was very interesting, but some of the jobs did not seem interesting at all. I remember watching a man whose job was to straighten the little blocks of cheese when they got twisted on a conveyer belt transporting tens of thousands of cheese chunks. He stood there all day with one hand near the conveyor. About every tenth block of cheese, he would reach forward and straighten it. That way the cheese would enter the wrapping machine properly and make its way to market without spoiling.

I thought to myself: *I'm glad I'm not doing that.* I'm not saying, of course, that the man was not doing good work or even holy work. It may have been both, but it did not seem like a job with much purpose in a world of far greater problems than misaligned chunks of cheese.

What actually makes our work significant before God? One of the ways we can assess our work is to use the George Bailey test. Do you remember the movie *It's a Wonderful Life*?[2] In that movie, the main character, George Bailey, considers ending his life because he doesn't think it's made any difference. The Lord sends an angel named Clarence, who is trying to "earn his wings," to show George what life would have been like if he had never been born. Throughout the rest of the movie, George discovers the amazing impact his life and work have had throughout the town of Bedford Falls.

I won't attempt here to correct all the theology of this senti-mental movie classic, but there are some legitimate takeaways. If we were to apply the George Bailey test to our work and what we produce, we would need to ask, "What would the world be like if we weren't doing our job?" For example, if there were no quality controls on the cheese factory assembly line, its product would spoil, its customers might get sick, and the business would lose its reputation. Without a good reputation, the business could no longer sell its products, so there would no longer be jobs available, and families could not be provided for.

These concerns take on added significance if we consider the importance of those doing quality control across the food industry, and across the drug industry, and across the nuclear waste industry, etc. The George Bailey test helps us understand that quality control is not just about the adjustment of cheese blocks but also making sure sanitation, safety, and security are maintained so that people don't get sick (with possible loss of a father or mother or child) and businesses don't get ruined (with possible loss of jobs, related businesses, and community).

As we examine our jobs with these perspectives, we begin to recognize that God is giving us the opportunity to fit our work into his present and future purposes. When we have that perspective, we realize that our work is not just about us but about its effects on others.

Making the World a Better Place

One of the people whose thoughts about work I most appreciate is David Wright. He became a college president after serving as a missionary in Haiti. Wright wrote a wonderful book called *How God Makes the World a Better Place*, which is about his experience in Haiti—a book made more poignant by recent difficulties in that nation. Wright said this:

> I saw [the purpose of every profession while I was] in Haiti. . . . Without a fair and dependable court system that ensured . . . honesty, fairness, and ownership . . . , Haitians struggled to turn their creativity and hard work into value for themselves, their families, or for their fellow Haitians. . . .
>
> Without a banking system that ensured that money could be protected and . . . borrowed on fair and workable terms to build small businesses, Haitians did not have the working

capital to . . . provide for their own needs and provide the goods and services their neighbors needed.[3]

Some of you are in the banking industry. Others are in legal services. Some of you are part of the educational system. If each of you were not doing your job, what impact might that have on others' families, churches, and communities?

By considering the downstream impact of our labors, each of us can gratefully kneel before God to say, "I'm beginning to understand. I'm not just a cog in a wheel somewhere. I've been given a holy calling, because God has called me to make a difference in the world he is building." God is making the world a better place, and he's doing it through people who work faithfully in his name.

Colossians 3:22 affirms that understanding. There Paul writes: "Bondservants [or slaves], obey in everything those who are your earthly masters, not by way of eye-service, as people-pleasers, but with sincerity of heart, fearing the Lord." When the apostle talks about "fearing the Lord," he has in mind a holy reverence, an attitude of honoring God.

Even slaves, whose work could be so unjust and demeaning (and whose situation can never be defended by a full reading of Scripture), were not being cut out of the opportunity to fulfill God's purposes. No matter how ignoble their position or task, all persons were being called to honor God—not by doing good work only when someone was watching, but by working for God's purposes even when he was the only one watching.

I once read a story about an entrepreneur who tried to set up a business in a developing country. The people there were not well educated, and they were very superstitious. Things went well for a time, and then workers began to take advantage of their boss when he wasn't watching them. So the boss decided to take advantage of their superstition.

He took out his glass eye and put it up on a shelf when he left the room, intending for the workers to believe he was watching them. This worked for a while, until the workers thought to put a hat over the glass eye.

Obviously, we can't put a hat over God's eye. He always sees us and is never blind to our efforts or situations. He is watching to provide whatever is necessary to accomplish his purposes through our practices and to extend his blessings through our products. Knowing this, we seek to serve him and not just our earthly bosses. No matter how challenging or mundane our duties, our job is holy before God because it is contributing to the world he is building for his own purposes. So, we work to honor God at all times and with our whole heart. We are called to strive for excellence, not simply for our recognition or reward but for the advancement of the glory and goodness of Christ.

Finding Fulfillment in Christ

We may think to ourselves: Such a calling sounds noble and good and will really help motivate us *when we get the job we want.* But is that the right perspective? We're in a society where we often talk about people choosing their calling. Young people are encouraged to ask, "What am I wired to do? What are my talents? What are my gifts? And where can I find a job that I enjoy in the area of my gifts so that I'll be fulfilled?"

I am not criticizing the impulse to seek a job that fits our personalities and talents, but the apostle Paul emphasizes something different. What if you have to work in a job that you don't want to do, with people who are difficult, and with duties not suited to your gifts? Paul calls us to recognize that our work is still a way of professing Christ, even if our vocation is not our choosing.

How do I know that's the case? Look again at Colossians 3:22: "[Slaves], obey in everything those who are your earthly masters." In North American culture, we tend to think that if we get enough education, if we work hard enough, and if we get to know the right people, then we will be able to find a fulfilling job that matches our gifts and talents.

That's not the case in most of the world or in most of world history. Instead, if your dad was a farmer, you became a farmer. If your dad was a miner, you became a miner. If your dad was a slave, you became a slave. Your rank, your caste, your race, your economic condition, your educational background, your nationality, and your demography were all predetermined.

Many people in our society still face similar situations. As racial inequities persist, as economic pressures increase, as layoffs occur, many never get jobs they desire, and many others have to leave jobs they love. Harsh realities put before us this basic question: Can I do what God wants if I can't do what I want? And God is telling us in Colossians 3:22, "Yes, even if you cannot do what you want, you can still do what I want."

I'm focusing on this verse for a number of reasons. First, it starts with the word *bondservants*, or *slaves*. We may be wondering why Paul isn't abolishing slavery rather than telling slaves how to work. That is a complex question and one that would take more than a few paragraphs to explore. But for now, we should note that in the very next chapter of Colossians, Paul says things that chop away at the roots of slavery as an institution.

In Colossians 4:1 Paul says, "Masters, treat your bondservants [slaves] justly and fairly, knowing that you also have a Master in heaven." He goes even further in his letter to Philemon, where he talks about the runaway slave Onesimus: "He was separated from you for a little while . . . that you might have him back forever—no longer as a slave, but better than a slave, as a dear brother" (Philem. 15–16 NIV).

Paul's most far-reaching statement about slavery is in Galatians 3:27–28: "For as many of you as were baptized into Christ have put on Christ. There is neither Jew nor Greek, there is neither slave nor free, there is no male and female, for you are all one in Christ Jesus." Paul's writings undermine all the presumptions that support any form of slavery, which denies human dignity and rights.

Still, since some of Paul's readers were slaves, he reminds them that they serve a higher authority. Their ultimate devotion is not to their earthly masters but to God himself: "Whatever you do, work heartily, as for the Lord and not for men" (Col. 3:23). The apostle's goal was not to preserve inequities but to promote the kingdom of the God who will eradicate all oppression and injustice. Our God never endorses oppression or fails to use the faithful efforts of his people when they must endure or oppose it. You can be in an undesirable job and still do God's work, because you're not serving men but the Lord.

Howard Hendricks, a longtime professor at Dallas Seminary, was on an American Airlines flight when he observed a flight attendant who was handling a drunk businessman, a screaming set of babies, and several unruly and unkind passengers.

Despite the challenges, she was treating all the passengers with politeness and courtesy. Hendricks asked her as he was leaving the plane, "Can I write a note to your supervisor at American Airlines?" And she replied, "Well, sure, you can do that." But then she said, "I don't actually work for a boss at American Airlines. My boss is Jesus Christ."

Of course, I'm not asking you to go in to work tomorrow and say to your boss, "I don't actually work for you," but I want you to know it in your heart. Your true Master, the one that you're ultimately serving, is the Lord himself. For that reason, if someone asks you to do something that's unethical or ungodly or unfair— even if your earthly boss believes he or she has that authority—you should remember that person is not your ultimate supervisor. We never have to obey commands that are contrary to God's will, because we serve Jesus Christ above all others.

Our Highest Priority in the Workplace

If we're working for the Lord and not for men, that also means we're not ultimately working for ourselves either. There's a higher priority than you in the workplace.

That becomes very important to know in a variety of pressure-packed situations. On occasion we may think, *Am I willing to transgress what I know God requires in order to get a promotion or a bigger salary or the approval of my boss?* If that's the case, then we need to be reminded that we are serving the Lord and not ourselves.

Scripture makes it clear that we are also called to serve our loved ones through our work. In our culture, where many jobs are hard and opportunities are decreasing, people are having to do things they don't want to do—jobs that aren't related to their gifting or talents. But ringing in our ears should be the words of Paul in 1 Timothy 5:8, where he says, "If anyone does not provide for his relatives, and especially for members of his household, he has denied the faith and is worse than an unbeliever."

Sometimes we say, "But I want to do what I like. I want to do what fulfills me." When those thoughts cross our minds, we also need to ask, "What is right for my family? Do I need to do things that are undesirable or unpleasant because taking care of my family is the clear calling and responsibility God has given me?" You may need to thank God that you have a job and are able to provide for your family, even if it's not the job of your dreams.

My father made a decision reflecting these principles when I was in high school and my parents were in deep tension with each other. He had an opportunity to go to another state and take a regional directorship for his company. He turned the position down. He explained his decision in private to me and my brothers: "Because of the way things are between your mom and me right now, this family needs the stability of staying here. I'm not going to take that promotion."

The job would have been great for him and for his career, and it would have paid more money. But my father recognized he had a higher calling. God wanted him to provide for his family in the way that was best and most appropriate for their welfare and long-term good.

God calls all of us to similar responsibility: to recognize that our work is more than a job to do; it is a divine calling. That calling involves honoring God first, even if it means we cannot do the things we would prefer to do for our own benefit. God's calling supersedes our personal preferences.

The Heart of Our Profession

Honoring God also means pursuing our profession from the heart. Paul emphasizes this in Colossians 3:23–24, writing, "Whatever you do, *work heartily*, as for the Lord and not for men, knowing that from the Lord you will receive the inheritance as your reward." The word "heartily" is not from the Greek word for "heart" but rather from the word we ordinarily translate as "soul." As we serve God through our work, we are to respond out of the depth of our soul.

Serving God heartily is not based upon how many toys we can get or how easy our lives can be. Instead, we do what he requires because of our deep-down, soul-level love for him. Remember Colossians 3:17: "Whatever you do, in word or deed, do everything in the name of the Lord Jesus, giving thanks to God the Father through him." We honor and give thanks to God because he sent his Son to earth and provided his life for us.

This God-glorifying gratitude is not only based on Christ's *past* provision. Colossians 3:24 goes on to say that you gain motivation from "knowing that from the Lord you will receive the inheritance as your reward. You are serving the Lord Christ." Here, Paul tells us that we *will receive* a lasting inheritance from the Lord in heaven that should make us willing to do hard things for him in this life.

In other words, Paul is calling us to have an eternal perspective. We should recognize that this life is short. There may be hard things here, but we're actually living for a far greater glory that goes on eternally.

That may sound good when you're at home reading this book. But it will be harder when you've got a difficult business decision to make or a difficult person to face. At those times, remember that you are living so as to express thanks for the Lord Christ—the King of creation, the Lord of all things, who brought your life, your family, and this world into existence.

He is also the Christ, the anointed one, who voluntarily died on the cross for your sin. He is with you in this situation, and—no matter what happens in the present—he has already provided an eternal inheritance that will make this present difficulty minuscule. He already has good plans for you on the other side of this trial or affliction. For the long term, you have nothing to lose by doing what honors your God in this moment.

Driven by Gratitude

These biblical principles are directing our hearts to be driven by eternal gratitude more than earthly gain. Our hearts should respond to Christ's cross by saying, "If he loved me so, then I want to live for him." That is what it means to be gospel driven.

When we realize that the Savior loved us enough to give himself for us and provide an eternal inheritance for us, we want other people to know that good news. When others see us sacrifice for the sake of our Savior, they understand his provision more. Just as Christ's sacrifice has touched our hearts, God intends for our sacrifice to touch others' hearts for Christ's sake. After all, we bear his name as Christians.

That's our calling: to make sure that the profession of our faith is apparent in our practices, in our products, and ultimately in our sacrifice for his purposes. Our heart's thankful response to his love motivates and enables us to honor him in the workplace, in our homes, in the easy places and in the hard places, with easy people and with difficult people. We do everything for Christ's sake, finding our greatest delight and deepest fulfillment in what makes his name glorious.

I have a friend named Casey who lives and works in Australia. A few years ago, Casey won an international architecture award for designing a home to fit into an abandoned and deteriorating space in a major Australian city. His design became a model for using rejected spaces and discarded materials in major cities around the world.[4] Because of that award, Casey and his wife, Rebekah, are now being asked to lecture and write in many professional settings about what motivates them, and what should motivate anyone in the field of architecture.

Recently, Casey wrote me about what they are doing. He and "Bek" were asked to give a lecture at a university on what it means to have architecture reflect their values. In his letter Casey said this:

> We presented our house design and discussed our architectural purpose, explored over twelve years of designing and building this home. We said we wanted to build this house, and houses like it, to show the blessings of Christ on restoring the rejected and to show his love as we serve others in our life and in our work.

Throughout the lecture, they explained how their vocation, their designs, and their work were meant to express the character and care of their Savior.

After the lecture, a young woman came up to them and said, "I have never heard anyone say how the gospel affects daily work and gives meaning to life." A man who had been an architect for a number of years also said: "That was a powerful moment in your lecture, because I have prayed for a decade for God to show me how to use my profession to bring light to a broken world."

What Casey and Rebekah were basically saying was this: "Show what you believe by the values your work expresses. Do your job with excellence, with integrity, and with compassion so that others may know the character and care of the God who made eternal provision for you." That's not always easy.

Casey recently turned down a billion-dollar contract to create a city design that he believed would cause people to be exploited for gambling profits. He was willing to sacrifice a very lucrative assignment for the sake of showing the world the heart of Jesus Christ. Casey rejoices now to see people hearing about his work and responding to what he has created. When he turned down the lucrative contract, he could not predict the results. Only later was he able to write, "As we have honored Christ, he has honored his own name in us."

That is the same privilege you have. God is calling you to a profession. His name is on you. Profess him in all you do. Honor him, and he will use your work for his purposes. *How* he will use you is beyond human prediction, but *that* he will honor himself in your work is his divine promise for all whose vocation is pursued for his name's sake.

3

Integrity

"YOU CALL THIS CLEAN? This is not quality work!"

A guard gave that review to Kenneth Bae, a long-held prisoner in North Korea and my former student. Bae's crime was simply to take believers with him into North Korea to pray for the people of that country. He did not smuggle any Bibles into the country and did not organize any evangelistic crusades. Yet when Bae's hotel room was searched and his prayer designs were discovered in notes on his computer, he was arrested. After a quick trial, Bae was sentenced to fifteen years of hard labor for unspecified crimes against the state.

In his book, *Not Forgotten*, Bae writes about that experience as a prisoner, including this exchange with a guard:

> "You call this clean? This is not quality work. Do this again!"
>
> "Okay," I said.
>
> [The guard] spun around on his boots. "How are you supposed to address me, 103? Is that how you are supposed to address me? You say it again correctly this time!"

"Yes, sir," I said.

"Did you have permission to speak, 103?" he snapped back.

"I am sorry. Excuse me, teacher. May I speak, please?" I said, still on the floor.

"Stand up when you speak to me," he said.

I stood up and repeated, "Excuse me, teacher. May I speak, please?" Having to call him teacher and sir felt very strange because I was old enough to be the guard's father.

"Yes, you may speak, 103."

"Yes, teacher, I will scrub the floor again," I said.[1]

After that experience and many similar ones, Bae writes, "I never argued or tried to defend myself. I knew my words would never convince him that I was something other than what he'd already decided I was. Instead, I tried very hard to do my work well and to do it with the right attitude. I believed that if [the guards] could see a difference in me, then their hearts might soften."[2]

Despite the obscurity and difficulty of his work, Bae's goal was to labor in a way that would portray the heart of his Lord. Why? Years before, Bae had prayed for the Lord to use him as a bridge connecting North Korea to the outside world and to God's word.[3]

He never imagined that his prayer would result in a fifteen-year sentence to a hard labor camp. Yet that was the place and the work that God intended for him. So even there, Bae worked with integrity, believing that God could use honest and diligent labor as a testimony. The conditions were terrible and unfair, but Bae believed the testimony of integrity was his to give for God's purposes. Then it was up to the Lord to use that testimony in whatever way he chose.

Ultimately God used the severity and length of Bae's sentence to shine his faith across the world. When he became the longest-held American in North Korean captivity, political pressures made his plight international news. The world focused attention on Bae; he turned the attention to Christ. Bae's testimony of integrity became God's instrument for answering Bae's "bridge prayer" in ways greater than he could ever have asked or imagined.

The Impact of Integrity

We want to ask, "Why did God allow Kenneth Bae to experience such hardships? What difference does it make to live with integrity before a watching world?" Those are important questions, whether you are in a labor camp, on the assembly line, in construction work, in an office, at school, on a farm, in a nursing home, or nursing a baby.

To answer that question, we first need to define what *integrity* is. Normally, the word means "the quality of being honest and having strong moral principles."[4] That definition is reflected in Psalm 15:4: a blameless person is one "who swears to his own hurt and does not change." In other words, he's true to his word and fulfills his obligations, even if the circumstances change, and even if there's an unexpected cost. A person of integrity is trustworthy under pressure, and his words and actions are true despite the pressure.

The Lord wants us to have integrity because that's his nature too. Psalm 25, on which most of the thoughts of this chapter are based, says, "Good and upright is the LORD" (v. 8). Then the psalmist says in verse 21 of that same chapter how that nature is reflected in us: "May integrity and uprightness preserve me." The psalmist is praying, "Lord, if this is what you are like, then please let me shine a light on you by making me like you and preserving me in and for this testimony. Because you're upright, may I also be upright, willing to put my well-being into your hands by living consistently for you."

If we bear on us the name of Christ, then we will want our work to reflect his nature. That means being willing to ask the question, "If Christ were to do my job, how would he do it?" Integrity means working such that the nature of our work is in harmony with the nature of our God.

When Christ's nature and our work's character match, we adorn the name of our Savior with the qualities of our labor. *Adorn* is an old word. It means to make beautiful or attractive. If our God is to be beautiful or attractive to the watching world and our own hearts, he must be seen as true and trustworthy. And if we are adorning his nature and name with the qualities of our work, then it must be true and trustworthy as well.

There is a clear biblical purpose for such integrity. Look again at Psalm 25:8, which says, "Good and upright is the LORD; therefore he instructs sinners in the way." God's character contrasts with the way that sinners live. So when we reflect him, we instruct them.

A testimony of integrity is a powerful tool, but that does not mean it is easy to employ. It can be strongly opposed by those resisting God's influence in their lives. The psalmist also makes this clear, saying, "Consider how many are my foes, and with what violent hatred they hate me" (25:19). God designs the testimony of integrity to instruct those who hate whatever and whoever represents him. Integrity requires that we honestly face its challenges.

The Risk of Integrity

To live with integrity in the world is to put ourselves at risk. Yet we are called to reflect God's character through our lives regardless of the cost. Kenneth Bae exhibited that willingness when he spoke of the difficulty of staying true to God's will and ways when cruelty, injustice, and absolute fatigue would hit him. He wrote:

I sat in the complete darkness of my cell and sang love songs of Jesus. I was so tired I could not even open my eyes. My body ached, yet I thanked God for letting me endure another day. . . .

The guards, I knew, were listening. . . . A guard came to me privately [and] asked, "Pastor, what benefit would I get if I believe in God like you?" I think he knew the answer just from the song he had heard me sing. Then he asked, "What price do I have to pay to believe in God like you? What will it cost me?" I explained that there is no financial cost. However, to believe in Jesus means surrendering all to him.

Then came the final question, the one that I could tell bothered him the most. "If God is real, why are you still here? You have been here longer than any other prisoner."

I answered honestly. I told the guard that it was God's plan for me to be there, and that plan includes him and the other guards. "Without me, how would you hear about God and Jesus, his Son?"[5]

In Bae's "bridge prayer" he had said, "Lord, make me a bridge. Use my life in the way that you see fit, to make me a bridge to those around me. Fair or unfair, evil or good, make me a bridge."[6]

One of the ways God answered Bae's prayer was to enable him to live with integrity before those who persecuted him, who needed to know of his Savior. By integrity believers demonstrate both God's character and our confidence in his ultimate provision. We live with integrity before the watching world, because we want others to know our Savior and to know that he can be trusted even if it costs us while we are in the world.

Knowing God Better

Of course, we live with integrity not only for the benefit of the watching world. Our own hearts know God better through our integrity. Psalm 25 also says:

> Make me to know your ways, O Lord;
>   teach me your paths.
> Lead me in your truth and teach me,
>   for you are the God of my salvation;
>   for you I wait all the day long. (vv. 4–5)

Then verse 20 adds, "Oh, guard my soul, and deliver me!" These verses make the profound statement that when we are living in ways consistent with the Lord's faithfulness, he becomes more real to us. *We* know him better by walking in his ways.

This is not really a mystery. What God is doing by our testimony of integrity is making himself real in our own hearts and lives.

When I was in college, I had the privilege of working every summer for the same road construction company. I was a resource and repair dispatcher. After I'd done that job for a few summers, I developed a good relationship with my boss.

One day he said, "Bryan, you're doing a good job. I have a cabin a couple of hours from here. Why don't you go there for a couple of days? During the daytime, you can paint the cabin for me, and I'll keep you on the payroll. But during the evening, you can fish."

My brain quickly calculated: *I fish. You pay me. You bet!*

By that evening, I was at the cabin. Then I got a call from my father.

"Bryan, what are you doing?"

"Well, Dad, I got this great opportunity. If I paint this cabin in the daytime, I can fish at night, and I'm not losing any money."

My dad replied, "Bryan, what are you doing receiving company pay for private work?"

I hadn't thought of it that way. I didn't want to think of it that way.

I said to my father, "Dad, I can't go back to my boss and tell him that he's asking me to do something unethical. I need this job so that I can pay for tuition and stay in college."

My father said, "I know that you need a job. But I also know what you need for life, and this is not it."

So I left that night, went to my boss the next day, and told him that I could not do what he had asked of me. The conversation was tense, but he did not fire me.

I recognized in that moment that I could trust God when he called me to hard things, even if I did not want to face them. I learned that God was calling me to an ethical standard that was higher than my comfort zone. I praise God for my father, who made me stick to my faith. But I confess to you, it was hard—really hard—because you and I both know God's results are not always so obvious or immediate.

God calls us to integrity not just as a testimony to the watching world but to our own hearts. We are bringing the reality of our Savior into our lives when we say, "I will live for him, even when it is tough." At that moment, we are acting on the faith that God is preserving our spiritual good through the work we do with integrity—but such faith will inevitably face the challenges of an evil world (see Ps. 25:21). The psalmist is clear about the risks in his prayer: "Guard my soul, and deliver me" (v. 20). Why? Integrity is always praised but not always welcomed.

If you tell ordinary people in business or industry that integrity is good for business, they will agree. It preserves one's reputation and secures needed relationships. People are willing to do business with you when they know they can trust you.

For example, my wife and I are considering buying an appliance from a local company for the simple reason that we like the salesman in the commercial. He seems honest. Of course, he may not be honest, but we will probably go to his store because he appears to have integrity. Still, such business pragmatics will prove insufficient for maintaining biblical integrity that may require the sacrifice of profit, personal gain, or reputation. Sometimes we have to pray for God to show up when the profits don't. That's why the psalmist prays, "May integrity and uprightness preserve me, *for I wait for you*" (v. 21). He tells us that the results may not be immediate, and there may be negative consequences when we act with integrity. God may not be operating on our schedule.

The Consequences of Integrity

If we must wait for the Lord, if he's going to unfold his plan in the midst of troubles, enemies, and afflictions—which are also mentioned in Psalm 25—then it can be really tough to live with integrity. And, at times, it may not be good for business to live with integrity.

Between 2009 and 2016, Volkswagen, the largest car dealer in the world by sales, produced eleven million cars with software designed to deceive pollution test equipment. The environmental controls were so deceptive that the pollutants spewed by Volkswagen cars were as much as forty times the amount allowed by government regulations.[7]

During the time that Volkswagen was producing these cars with forty times the pollutants that were allowed, it was advertising itself as the greenest and most environmentally conscious of the major car dealers. How could such dishonesty go undetected for so long? There were two major explanations offered in later business journals.

One explanation was that executives at the very top of the company, with the complicity of hundreds if not thousands of workers, realized that the German economy required that Volkswagen do well. If the company did not do well, the impact upon the German economy would have been devastating. And if the German economy stumbled, then perhaps the entire world economy would suffer as a consequence. Therefore, the top executives at Volkswagen made a decision: it would be good for everyone in the long term if Volkswagen cheated for a short while.

Another explanation was also offered: a few engineers within the company determined that it was impossible to meet the antipollution standards with acceptable profit margins. Therefore, because the technology was not currently present to do as government standards required, the goal for the moment was to fake it until they could make it. The engineers simply reasoned that they would lose their jobs if they could not meet the standards that secured company profits. So they devised mechanisms to fake the needed results.

I don't know which explanation is true. But the facts illustrate that whether you are at the highest levels of decision-making or trying to keep your job, both levels of responsibility can experience extreme pressure to do what is unacceptable in Scripture—to deceive people to make a profit.

I have read the responses of managers at two major production and delivery companies who were surveyed about pressures in the workplace. Between 60 and 70 percent of the managers said they regularly had to compromise their integrity in order to succeed, or even survive, in their companies. Famous surveys done at major universities similarly revealed that between 60 and 70 percent of college students regularly cheat to get the grades they think they need to successfully enter the workforce. Apparently the patterns of compromise we adopt for success early in life become the default patterns for trying to attain later success and security.

With patterns of compromise so pervasive, living with integrity can be tough. Yet God requires it and promises to bless us through it. We need to embrace these truths early and regularly or we may soon establish life patterns that take us far from our God and from the character commitments that grant us self-respect and give him due honor.

Integrity Rescues Us from Uncertainty

Living with integrity is meant to rescue us from uncertainty. We often will find ourselves asking, *What should I do in this situation?*

But if the options are clear—a decision is either ungodly and unethical or true to God's word and ethical—then our choice should be clear.

Regardless of the consequences, if the ethical choices are clear, we do what the psalmist says: we take our refuge in God. In Psalm 25:20 the psalmist prays, "Guard my soul, and deliver me! Let me not be put to shame, *for I take refuge in you.*"

When I hear that word *refuge*, I think of a bomb shelter. If God is our bomb shelter, then it means that bombs are going to come. It means that life can be dangerous. But we also know that during those dangers we can rest safely in God's bomb shelter. We trust in his ultimate protection, saying: "You're the Creator of the universe. You're the one who controls all things. I recognize you've set the standards, and the world works best when we follow your standards. So, I'm going to take refuge in you and leave the results to you."

Wrestling with God's Word

Now, having said that living with integrity rescues us from uncertainty, I hope you realize that it doesn't mean the choice of paths is always simple. We live in a complex, fallen world, and sometimes we face difficult ethical dilemmas. Integrity is important not only when the options are clear, but also because it offers us the opportunity to wrestle with God's word when the options are not so clear.

Psalm 25:9 may surprise us a bit. It tells us that God "leads the humble in what is right, and teaches the humble his way." *Lead* and *teach* are both words of process, indicating that when the answers are not immediately clear, God helps us to find our way and teaches us along the way. There are times when we need to search and wrestle with God's word. We also need to seek Christian counsel and pray for the guidance of the Holy Spirit, saying: "God, I have to depend upon you because this decision is not obvious and is beyond my own wisdom. Help me to search deeply into your word and ways to find out what you're calling me to do."

Pastor Tim Keller tells an account of a man who came to him for advice. The man was an investment counselor for a major equity firm, and the team he worked with discovered a company they could invest in that would turn a huge profit very quickly. The problem was not the investment opportunity but the product of that company. Although the product was not illegal, it was not something that a Christian could support. The investment counselor said to Keller something like this:

> My whole team is recommending this investment to the company. If that particular company that we would be investing in made a lot of money, there wouldn't just be profit to me: there would be profit to the whole team. There would be bonuses for people. Our company would thrive. There would be more maximized value of shareholder holdings if our company did it. Everybody would do better. But I did not want to invest my life; I did not want to give advice to go to that company whose product I felt was against my own standard.[8]

What did the man do? At some point, he said this: "I cannot for the sake of my scruples hold these other team members back from what they think can benefit investors. It's not illegal what my team is pursuing. But neither can I in good conscience benefit from that investment." So the man told his team, "If this makes money, I will accept no profit from it. I will accept no bonus from it."

That may seem like an inadequate answer. But we're not in his situation. And we should realize that it's often easier to *imagine* what others should do when we are not in their shoes. What I ask you to recognize in that story was the man's willingness to struggle, to wrestle with the meaning of integrity in that situation, and to take a stand for his Savior. Over and over again, God provides us with opportunities in a fallen world to experience his teaching and guidance.

Waiting for God

Psalm 25 nears its conclusion with strange words: "May integrity and uprightness preserve me, *for I wait for you*" (v. 21). In essence, the psalmist is saying, "God, you may have to unfold this. I'm waiting to see what you will do." I think of similar words written by the prophet Habakkuk:

> The vision [of what God will do] awaits its appointed time. . . .
> If it seems slow, wait for it;
> > it will surely come; it will not delay. (Hab. 2:3)

Sometimes we must wait to witness the hand of God.

When I was in seminary, one of my very good friends was being put through seminary by his wife. She had a good salary as a quality control inspector for a major pharmaceutical company in St. Louis. Government regulations dictated that she alone had the credentials to authorize the safety and sale of certain products. One day a set of syringes that had been manufactured by her company went through quality inspection, and she found out that the entire lot was contaminated. Her boss quickly did the math. He realized that if they had to remanufacture this lot of syringes, the losses were going to be huge. So he said to my friend's wife, "Sign that the syringes are not contaminated." She said she could not do that. Her boss replied, "I'll give you the weekend to think about it. But if you will not sign on Monday morning, you're done at this company."

There was a lot of prayer that weekend. Monday morning came, and she did not sign. So she was fired. Losing her job put the couple into financial jeopardy, and their future in ministry was also threatened. Although it may have seemed like the wrong decision, the couple determined to wait on the Lord.

As it turned out, the company for whom the syringes were intended found out about the delay, found out who had caused the delay, and why. Then they hired her! They wanted her skills *and* her integrity.

Suffering for the Savior

Of course, we would not be honest if we said that life always works so neatly in a broken world. We need to recognize that there are greater benefits from our struggles than a guaranteed happy and immediate ending. Integrity in the workplace may give us opportunity to suffer for the Savior. Listen to what the apostle Paul says in Philippians 1:29: "It has been granted to you that for the sake of Christ you should not only believe in him but also suffer for his sake."

I don't like that.

Nobody does.

But remember what Christ has done for us. He voluntarily gave up his glory, coming to earth in the form of a servant. And then he suffered an agonizing death on the cross for our sins. Now he calls us to follow his example by suffering for the sake of others who are watching, who are aware that we are Christians. We willingly experience earthly and temporal suffering so that they might receive eternal life—which is exactly what our Savior did.

Kenneth Bae wrote of the difficulty of maintaining his commitment to integrity in the hard-labor camp:

> From the time of my arrest, I had meditated on all the promises of rescue in the Bible, especially in the psalms. *Does it mean God doesn't love me if he doesn't rescue me?* I wondered.
>
> I reread the letters I'd received from home, letters from my wife, my mother, my sister, and my children. The letters made them seem close and yet so much farther away. Is this the only way they are going to be able to know me for the next fifteen years? Is this the only contact I am going to get to have with everyone I love?
>
> I went back over the lines in my mother's last letter. "You are going to have to have the faith of Daniel's friends," she had said.
>
> Am I that strong? Can I do what they did? Can I keep trusting in God, even if the worst-case scenario comes true?
>
> For an entire week I wrestled with these questions. I prayed and prayed and asked God for wisdom and strength. My mood jumped between depressed and not quite as depressed. I sang sad songs, like the old Elvis tune "Are You Lonesome Tonight?"

and Eric Carmen's "All by Myself." To be honest, I really started feeling sorry for myself.

Finally, on September 24, 2013, I got down on my knees on my bed, and prayed.

Lord, you know my heart. You know what I want, but not my will but yours be done. You know I want to go home, but if you want me to stay, I will stay. I give up my right to go home. I surrender it to you. Please take care of my wife and my children and my parents. Please take care of them while you keep me here. If this is where you want me to be, okay. I embrace that as your will.

Then he wrote,

Peace came over me as a weight lifted off my shoulders.

God's Spirit filled the room and reminded me of my calling.

"I am a missionary," I said. "Lord, I am a missionary, and this is the mission field you have given me. Use me."

The moment I stopped praying, *God save me*, and instead prayed, *God, use me*, I felt free.[9]

God is calling us all to this kind of freedom. Similar to Kenneth Bae, we need to pray:

God, I'm not just asking you to save me for the moment. I want you to use me in the way that you think is best and right. I don't know what the earthly consequence may be, but I want to live for your sake. And for your sake, I am willing to sacrifice the temporal good of my own life, so that those around me, and my own soul, may know the eternal Savior better.

Such prayer enables us to recognize and fulfill the ultimate goal of the testimony of integrity: pointing everyone to the Savior.

Our Need for Grace

How can we live that way? How can we do all that God is calling us to do? We need to remember the words of Psalm 25:7: "Remember not the sins of my youth or my transgressions." In essence the psalmist is saying, "God, I'm not depending on my integrity to rescue me. I am fully aware of my great need for your forgiveness and aid. So, I am depending on you."

I could not help but laugh when I read an excerpted article from the *Harvard Business Review*, where a very bright person named Michael Schrage said in response to Volkswagen's cheating, "I believe Volkswagen's debacle signals the likely end of deliberate corporate malfeasance."[10] Are you kidding me? Has he ever heard of the Enron scandal? Or WorldCom, or Lehman Brothers, or Wells Fargo, or HealthSouth, or Swissair, or . . . The list began long before VW and will lengthen as long as profits trump scruples. Can he really believe that one major revelation of scandal is going to bring about the end of corporate malfeasance? Obviously, he doesn't understand Paul's words: "All have sinned and fall short of the glory of God" (Rom. 3:23).

I'm not just talking about people out there somewhere.

I'm talking about my heart.

I'm talking about your heart.

I'm talking about the pressures every one of us faces to hit the numbers, to meet the goals, to maintain the relationships, to get the dollars. As pressures mount, our regular temptation is to color the truth or twist it—to compromise integrity.

It is so easy to do.

And God is saying, "If I'm calling you to this standard, I hope you begin to recognize how much you need me."

Psalm 25 ends so wisely. In verse 22 the psalmist prays: "Redeem Israel, O God, out of all his troubles." This verse reminds us that because we struggle so much in a broken world that rewards deceit, we need a Redeemer. We need one to whom we can cry out, "Remember not the sins of my youth or my transgressions. . . . For your name's sake, O LORD, pardon my guilt, for it is great" (vv. 7, 11).

Gratitude to Our Savior

We also live with integrity to show our gratitude to our Savior for such pardon. By our integrity, we're not gaining grace but responding to it. When we truly understand that, then we rejoice at the mighty hand of God. We also begin to see God working around us in ways that we can't always explain, so we can say, "He is my Redeemer and I'm going to trust in him, even when I cannot anticipate what may come."

In that hard-labor camp, Kenneth Bae had one very unusual task. He was required to raise his own food. For a man who had never been a farmer, that was a difficult task, and they gave him an awful plot of land on a hillside to do it. It was exhausting for a man with health problems, including diabetes, to stand in the hot sun and try to break the hard dirt with a hoe.

One day, the camp commander chided him, pointing to his struggling, ragged little crops on the hillside and how they contrasted the prison's cultivated crops in neat rows in the valley below. The commandant said, "You have your help from heaven;

we have an agricultural system from Kim Il-Sung, our supreme leader. Look at the difference." Later Bae wrote:

> That night thunder and flashes of lightning woke me up. I heard rain pouring down. Then I heard some sort of commotion from inside the building. People were yelling, and I heard footsteps running up and down the hallway and the outside door slamming. I was too tired to get up and look out my window. Instead I rolled over and went back to sleep.
>
> The next morning I saw the warden go past my room, visibly upset. "What happened?" I asked.
>
> "There was a flood last night. The entire bean field is underwater. It's all lost," he said. This was a huge blow because these beans were supposed to feed the guards and the rest of the staff.
>
> When I went outside, I noticed everything was not lost. The guards' field was washed away—but my field was fine. I felt a little like the Israelites when the plagues hit Egypt but left them alone.
>
> I smiled and prayed to myself, *Lord, you are really humorous. You sure made your point here!*[1]

The point is to show others Christ's character and care. As we bear his suffering and reflect his nature, we say to the world, "I trust my Savior so much that I will give myself with integrity to his purposes. When I fall, he'll pick me up and forgive me. And I'll keep on living for him, because he gave himself to secure eternal good for me."

4

Money

AN ALTERNATIVE COUNTRY BAND called The Dirty Guv'nahs honestly reflects in song about youthful longing for a luxury life that provides trinkets, travel, and opportunities to show off. The expensive things are supposed to grant happiness and control of what happens in life, but the song ends with a surprising note of a different longing when success and maturity come. The singers want a life free of the compulsion to obtain things that are supposed to make you happy.[1]

At the heart of this song is the recognition that the things we think we need, and all the expensive things for which we yearn, can bring bondage to our lives rather than freedom. And it's for that reason that the Lord Jesus speaks about the subject of money so frequently.

We sometimes forget how often Jesus talks about money. He talks about money more than he talks about hell. He talks about money more than he talks about heaven. One quarter of all the parables are about the subject of money.

Why does Jesus talk so much about money? It is because he knows that where our treasure is, there will our heart be also (Matt. 6:21). Jesus wants our heart to be free and united to him in the joy of the gospel. For this reason, he and his apostles care for us by regularly instructing us in the blessings and dangers of money.

The apostle Paul instructs us about rightly handling our resources in a very significant passage, 1 Timothy 5:8–18, which picks up right in the middle of a discussion about the church's responsibility to care for those in need:

> But if anyone does not provide for his relatives, and especially for members of his household, he has denied the faith and is worse than an unbeliever.
>
> Let a widow be enrolled if she is not less than sixty years of age, having been the wife of one husband, and having a reputation for good works: if she has brought up children, has shown hospitality, has washed the feet of the saints, has cared for the afflicted, and has devoted herself to every good work. But refuse to enroll younger widows, for when their passions draw them away from Christ, they desire to marry and so incur condemnation for having abandoned their former faith. Besides that, they learn to be idlers, going about from house to house, and not only idlers, but also gossips and busybodies, saying what they should not. So I would have younger widows marry, bear children, manage their households, and give the adversary no occasion for slander. For some have already strayed after Satan. If any believing woman has relatives who are widows, let her care for them. Let the church not be burdened, so that it may care for those who are truly widows.

Let the elders who rule well be considered worthy of double honor, especially those who labor in preaching and teaching. For the Scripture says, "You shall not muzzle an ox when it treads out the grain," and, "The laborer deserves his wages."

Later in 1 Timothy, Paul adds those famous words: "The love of money is a root of all kinds of evil" (1 Tim 6:10). Still, it's important to note that this caution about the potential evils of money follows what the apostle says can be good about money.

It can't be all bad, you know. Even the Lord himself says, "The laborer deserves his wages" (Luke 10:7). If Jesus says that wages are something people deserve, then money isn't necessarily evil.

But what good is money? In 1 Timothy 5:8–18, Paul identifies three good purposes of money, almost as case studies. He teaches that the church can use the blessings of money to provide for mercy, family, and ministry.

Money and Mercy

Widows are the focus of this passage, but in similar passages Jesus and the apostles talk about money in relation to others in disadvantaged circumstances: the poor, the imprisoned, refugees, the sick, and orphans. Many times the Lord tells us that the church and the people who have money should be using it to extend mercy to these persons in need. Why is mercy so important? It is important because it reflects the gospel. Mercy is about helping people who cannot help themselves and providing for those who cannot provide for themselves. That's a physical message, but it reflects the spiritual realities of God's grace by which he provides mercy, pardon, and heaven for those whose earning or effort could never secure them.

The gospel says to God's people, "When you cannot provide for your own holiness, for your own righteousness, and for your own eradication of sin, then God in his mercy provides for you through faith in Christ Jesus's work." Because God has shown mercy to those who cannot provide for themselves, the church's ministries of mercy become object lessons of this gospel of grace.

First Timothy 5:9 specifically directs the church to extend mercy to widows by instructing, "Let a widow be enrolled [on the mercy list] if she is not less than sixty years of age, having been the wife of one husband." In the churches of Paul's day, if a widow did not have anyone to provide for her, the church could put her on its "widow's list" and provide for her physical needs. That means that the church was providing for its people simply to express the gospel's message of the value and the dignity of individuals—not because they could give back to the church but simply because they were made in the image of God and had dignity before him.

We talked about this before in terms of our work. The reason we know that our work honors God is that we who do it are made in the image of God. Because God so dignifies us, the work of our hands has dignity. That does not mean that everything we produce is museum quality, but it is valuable to God because we are heaven-created and divinely treasured. That's easy to forget.

When I was a pastor in southern Illinois, I can remember a time when two women began to attend our church. They did not have any relatives in the church, and they did not have much money. One of the women got so depressed about their situation that she attempted suicide. That shook our church and got the attention of our elders. In one of the very honest discussions among our leaders, the question came up, "Why were we so unaware of these women and their plight while they've been attending our church?" One wise and compassionate elder replied very honestly, "The reason we did not know about them is that it was not to anyone's advantage to pay attention to them."

The church should show mercy not for anyone's advantage but because all who are created in God's image have dignity and worth. We reflect the gospel when we take care of those who cannot help themselves, showing our understanding of their worth to God even when they may have little of the world's resources or reputation.

In this passage Paul insists that all in the church should develop the grace of mercy. He wisely cautions his readers not to help those who have children or grandchildren who should support them, saying, "Let [their children or grandchildren] first learn to show godliness to their own household and to make some return to their parents, for this is pleasing in the sight of God" (5:4).

The apostle also warns against putting younger widows—those below the age of sixty—on the list. Such people with youthful energy but without earthly obligations may be tempted to spend time in other people's homes and in other people's business, becoming busybodies and slanderers. Paul is saying, "Church, make good use of your money. Help those who have legitimate needs. But don't help those who have other resources or whose dependence on the church will tempt them to become idle or immoral."

Authors Brian Fikkert and Steve Corbett have written an important book entitled *When Helping Hurts*.[2] They point out that some churches make unwise decisions about whom they serve. Instead of helping people to find their dignity in their work, the church maintains an unhealthy dependence rather than stimulating a dignifying independence.

Decisions about whom to help can be particularly hard in a society where there may be intergenerational poverty, long-term racism, and systemic injustice that make people unwilling or unable to find work. We may wonder: *What is our role here?*

Paul shows us both sides of the issue. On the one hand, the church should not be burdened with providing for those who have other means of support. On the other hand, the church has a duty to show mercy to persons in need in order to reflect the gospel. Our decisions should not be based on others' deserving (grace only for the deserving is not grace at all), but on the difference our expression of mercy can make for demonstrating, and helping others to embrace, the gospel.

I admire, and give thanks for, those churches that seriously consider the best ways to extend mercy to those in need, without creating barriers of deservedness that actually become excuses for stinginess. While concerns about others taking advantage of our benevolence justify wisdom in the distribution of mercy, they do not outweigh the necessity of generosity of spirit and resources for Christ's sake. The mercy we show gives credibility to the gospel we express and reshapes our world and that of others according to Christ's priorities.

Money and Family

The right use of money also reflects the gospel to our own families. That is why the apostle says, "If anyone does not provide for his relatives, and especially for members of his household, he has denied the faith and is worse than an unbeliever" (1 Tim. 5:8).

Paul isn't saying that our mercy somehow merits salvation. Rather, he makes it plain that our willingness to care for other people shows the hand and the heart of God to all people. If we are unwilling to do that, our own family's understanding of Christ can be damaged. A grasping and greedy expression of the gospel by a believer is worse than the testimony of an unbeliever.

Paul isn't just addressing heads of households in this passage. He says, "If a widow has children or grandchildren, let them first learn to show godliness to their own household and to make some return to their parents, for this is pleasing in the sight of God" (5:4). He goes on to say, "If any believing woman has relatives who are widows, let her care for them" (5:16).

Children, grandchildren, women of means, heads of household—a wide variety of family members are mentioned because it's so powerful a testimony of the gospel when God's people show selfless concern for others with the funds that God has given them. If such concern will not even be shown to one's own relatives, then the gospel seems worthless or worse to onlookers.

Unfortunately we sometimes overlook our financial responsibility to our family members. We might say to ourselves, *It's my money, so I have every right to provide for my own needs and desires.* But in thinking that way, the needs of others in our extended family are made incidental or inconsequential to us.

The apostle Paul is very clear here. Those who put self-indulgence above the needs of their families are worse than unbelievers because such selfishness is a contradiction of the gospel by the very ones who claim its truths. We are called to care for those who cannot take care of themselves, because God has done that for us in Christ. Failing to do that with our money denies what we believe no matter what our mouths attest.

Of course, there are many reasons why people may not provide for their families. Our self-indulgence may be due to inattention to others' needs or to some preoccupying addiction—alcoholism, gambling, workaholism, sports manias, or anything else that keeps us focused on ourselves rather than on our extended family. Such self-preoccupation never furthers the cause of the gospel *in* or *beyond* our homes.

Public schooling began as a movement within the church. Christians understood the dignity of all children made in the image of God. That understanding in an era of sweatshops and illiteracy convinced Christians that it was their responsibility to help educate future generations so that all children would have opportunities to share in our nation's blessings, enabling our entire society to flourish.

That sense of responsibility for others certainly cost believers a lot of time and money, and most of our nation has probably forgotten the sacrifice Christians made to found our school systems. Yet if we are concerned for both the spiritual and temporal needs of God's extended family, then we make such decisions for his children.

Because of the age range of our children, Kathy and I paid tuitions for Christian schools for over twenty-five consecutive years. Some people look at us and say, "You are crazy," but we reply, "What better way could we spend our money than on the spiritually sensitive education of our children?"

If heaven is real, and if the eternal good of our children is part of our responsibility, then we make decisions mindful of the earthly and eternal needs of those whom God has put in our households. Such decisions do not always include money, but they should not exclude how we use our money to bless those entrusted to our care. Christians recognize that money has been given to us by God for ministries of mercy *and* for the care of our families. Money rightly used advances understanding of and love for the gospel.

The gospel tells us that we are no longer strangers and aliens but fellow citizens and members of God's household (Eph. 2:19). He is our Father, and we cry out to him, "Abba, Father." How we steward family relationships and resources can and should reflect how dear and selfless is the heavenly Father's care.

In Roman society, many people were converted when they witnessed the selfless priorities and sacrificial care of Christian families. People raised in a self-promoting and licentious culture realized that they had never experienced that kind of love. They had never known compassion without conditions or an embrace that could not be jeopardized by failing to meet expectations. The value of valuing others above personal advantage that was exhibited in Christian families became a powerful presentation of the gospel.

When we are using our resources for the care of those in our family, whether we are children, grandchildren, widows, or heads of households, then we're reflecting the gospel as God intends.

Money and Ministry

In addition to addressing concerns of mercy and family, money should also be used for resourcing God's ministry. The apostle Paul says, "Let the elders who rule well be considered worthy of double honor, especially those who labor in preaching and teaching"

(1 Tim. 5:17). The expression "double honor" in biblical times referred to the financial provision, as well as the recognition of office, that people in the church were to give to those engaged in full-time preaching and teaching of God's word.

Paul explains, "For the Scripture says, 'You shall not muzzle an ox when it treads out the grain,' and, 'The laborer deserves his wages'" (5:18). The message: our money is supposed to provide for those providing the grain of the gospel for the spiritual nurture of others. Of course, this is a message that many Christians dread because it can make us feel guilty that we are not always generous in gospel purposes. But guilt is not Paul's goal.

Over many years of ministry, I have discovered that God's people want to support Christ's cause. Yes, they will struggle with priorities, but they want to be a part of God's mission. They actually long for this.

I have spent a lot of my life asking people for money. Because of my positions as pastor, seminary president, and denominational leader, I have asked some of the wealthiest people in the world for money. Over time, I have also learned to recognize two distinct categories of persons by their responses to my requests.

One group has discovered the joy of giving. They understand that their money can have an eternal impact, and they view themselves as stewards undeservedly, even inexplicably, blessed with earthly resources for the advance of eternal purposes. They are well aware that there are others more intelligent, godly, and savvy who have not been blessed with a similar convergence of circumstances that accounts for personal wealth. So they believe that God in his grace has specially chosen and enabled them to bless his people and further his objectives. Though they cannot give to everybody, these grateful and humble stewards delight to advance causes that they believe will promote the priorities of their Savior.

The second group is willing to give money, but they do so grudgingly. Such people seem to want me to approach them as a beggar even though I believe that I am on a holy errand, seeking resources to support God's mission in the world. I confess that there have been times that I have wanted to retort to a demeaning comment from a wealthy patron, "Don't you dare treat me so dismissively. I am no beggar. I am a child of the King."

A pastor friend of mine who also needed occasionally to ask God's people for funds for critical mission projects tried to help me deal with this second group of Christian givers by telling me a story. He said, "I went to a wealthy man, and he stiff-armed me because he did not want to give. Yet he told me, 'Oh, pastor, when we get to eternity, you're going to be so pleased to find out how much money I've given to the Lord.'" The pastor replied, "After you have been in eternity for three seconds, you will grieve that you did not triple your gifts."

Although that sounds sort of spiritual and satisfying to my resentments, it is totally untrue. When you get to heaven, you will not feel guilty about anything, because Christ will have forgiven you of every selfish and stingy sin. It's that great provision of our Savior that should motivate us to give now out of gratitude for the gospel that saved us and for the joy of spreading it. All Christians are called to give to God's purposes out of thanksgiving for his grace, not to relieve their guilt. Jesus takes guilt away; giving money does not. Guilt never promotes healthy giving; joy always does.

Joyful giving is possible because we believe that God is using our wealth, our resources, and our stewardship for eternal purposes. We rejoice to be privileged to participate in God's mission.

The man who helped me the most in my fundraising was Ben Edwards, who was the head of the A. G. Edwards investment company. He gave a lot of money to Christian causes around the world. When I went to him as a new seminary president, I didn't know how to raise money.

I asked, "Ben, how do you do this?"

He replied, "It's not that difficult. Tell God's work to God's people, and let God take care of the rest."

I loved that, and I realized that I could do as he suggested.

Christian leaders have such a wonderful privilege to talk about God's work to God's people and then watch as God does his work among us. When you experience that privilege, it changes you. You discover that making requests for ministry purposes is not about twisting arms; it's about rejoicing that God is able to use people like us to steward what he has given for amazing, eternal purposes.

If God is changing eternity through money given for mercy, family, and ministry, then why do we so struggle to give? It's because we have trouble seeing the great privileges we have. It's so much easier to see our earthly loss than to envisage heaven's gain. That's why I need to emphasize that discussions about money should not focus entirely on resourcing God's purposes. Ultimately, a healthy approach to money is about revealing our privileges.

Money and Privilege

What privileges does money provide? One important privilege is that we have been granted our daily bread through money.

The fact that we have daily bread is intended to release us from fear. We don't have to go through every day wondering if we are going to make it.

My wife's father used to tell us a story about a couple he knew in college. They married while they were still in school and struggled to get by financially every month. To assure themselves that they could make it through the month, they kept thirty-one cans of pork and beans on their pantry shelves. That way, no matter what happened that month, they knew they would have a meal of pork and beans available for each day. They might not eat well or party at the Ritz, but they would not starve!

What does it mean when you and I have the money for mercy and family and ministry and daily bread (or pork and beans)? Think about the words from James 1:17: "Every good gift and every perfect gift is from above, coming down from the Father of lights, with whom there is no variation or shadow due to change." We can buy groceries, go to Walmart, or even go to the soup kitchen if we are hungry because the same hand that created the lights of the sky—sun, moon, and stars—is operating in your life and mine. We have money for daily bread because the King of the universe is active in our lives.

If we really believe that the God who created the universe cares for us and is working in our lives, then that removes the fear that makes us hoard our money and turn away everyone who might need the generosity that God asks of us.

God's daily provision also reminds us that our security is not in our bank accounts. Every now and then as the stock market plunges, I lose a lot of money in my retirement account. I've discovered that when I lose so much money, I can actually become more generous. Why? It's because if one of my children then comes to me and says, "Dad, I need some money for a car repair," or, "I need help with college tuition," I think to myself, *I've already lost so much, what difference does a little more subtraction make?* So awareness of my inability to protect my "stash" makes me more ready to share it. And my confidence of God's abiding care, despite my immediate loss, makes me more ready to trust him for all my real needs.

When God teaches us that our security is in him and not in our bank account, that allows us to be free from fear. Such fearlessness enables us to put our lives and resources on the line for Jesus. Our attitude toward our money—when we remember the Lord is our ultimate security—can free us for selfless and courageous service. We sometimes forget that God provides money as a kind of holy compass for our lives. How we view money (whether we are its stewards or its hostages) is an indicator of whether our hearts are in line with, or off course from, God's mission.

Money and Contentment

Of course, Paul also tells us in 1 Timothy 6:10 that "the love of money is a root of all kinds of evils." But that verse comes in the context of God reminding us that "godliness with contentment is great gain" (6:6). Paul goes on to say that "it is through this craving that some have wandered away from the faith and pierced themselves with many pangs" (6:10).

We sometimes think to ourselves, *I want more. What I have isn't enough.* And Paul tells us, "Because you're not content and are always wanting more, you're actually hurting yourself." If we were content, we could pray the prayer of Proverbs 30:8–9:

Give me neither poverty nor riches;
 feed me with the food that is needful for me,
lest I be full and deny you
 and say, "Who is the LORD?"
or lest I be poor and steal
 and profane the name of my God.

God knows our personalities; he knows our needs; he knows our souls; he knows what tempts us; he knows what supports us. So he gives us just the right balance between poverty and riches. If you knew for sure that God was providing—to the penny—what you needed to glorify him, you would be content.

How can we tell when we've drifted off the path of content-ment? One way is when we experience envy. We think to ourselves, *I want what they have, Lord, not what you're providing.* We become discontent when driven by consumer culture and by our sinful nature to want more than what God supplies: *I've got to have that kind of car. I've got to have that big house. I've got to have those clothes. I've got to take that expensive vacation.*

Often the evidence of our envy is our debt. A survey from a few years ago revealed that the average credit card debt in the United States was $17,000. The average auto loan debt was $30,000. The average mortgage debt was $182,000 (it's now over $200,000). And the average student loan debt was $51,000.[3] I recognize the last two can be called "investment debt" rather than "consumer debt," but the cumulative effect is families feeling absolutely crushed by debt.

The same news report said half of all American families are embarrassed by their debt. I'm not so concerned about our embarrassment as I am about our imprisonment—shackles of debt that make us sleepless and stressed and hurting and fearful of creditors in ways that rob us of the joy of our salvation. That's not the freedom from fear and want that God wants us to have.

Perhaps the greatest evidence that we are not content is when we lose our generosity. We say to ourselves, *I can't do more. I can't provide for those who need mercy, I can't provide for my extended family, and I can't provide for ministry—at least not very much.* If we have lost the capacity for generosity, contentment is gone too. During such times, God is saying to us, "There are people who need mercy. There is family who needs your care. There is a ministry that needs your support."

If you knew that your funds were supporting people who need mercy, then you would earn all you could. If you knew that your funds were providing for the security of your family, you would save all you could. And if you knew that your funds were providing for the ministry of the gospel, you would give all you could. That's why John Wesley said, "Earn all you can, save all you can, give all you can."

Money and Giving

Many of us have been taught about tithing (i.e., dedicating a tenth of our income to God's purposes). But often those who preach about tithing point back to the temple tithe in the Old Testament, and they forget that it was just one of the tithes God required for the people of Israel. There were temple tithes, priestly tithes, tithes for the poor, and tithes for the feast days. There were also sacrifices and Passover feasts that had to be paid for. And we shouldn't forget the year of jubilee, when all debts were canceled, and all land went back to the original owner.

So are we required to tithe today? The only place in the New Testament where a tithe is specifically mentioned is where Jesus criticized the Pharisees and the scribes for tithing mint and cumin (their spices) while ignoring the weightier matters of the law: justice, mercy, and faithfulness. Jesus tells these "law keepers" not to neglect their tithes (applicable under the Old Testament codes they were living), but to move beyond legalism to love of God's people and purposes as motivation (see Matt. 23:23).

God is calling us to give from the heart, because if we begin to establish legalistic rules for giving, we will begin to argue over our rules rather than assessing others' needs. Are we supposed to tithe on the gross or the net? Should we tithe before taxes or after taxes? Should we tithe on the investment value, the purchase value, or the market value? I have heard preachers and accountants try to argue such things from the scantiest of biblical evidence in ways that make me blush.

What's a better, more biblical way for New Testament Christians to think? Here's where I land out of love for Christ and zeal for God's mission: if those anticipating the gospel in Old Testament times gave one-tenth of their income, how much more should we, who fully know the triumph of our risen Lord and the goodness of his gospel, be willing to give for Christ's purposes? God wants our generosity to be motivated by gratitude and thanksgiving for who he is and what he has done.

An honest tithe can be a good marker of a generous heart, but selfless hearts that are sensitive to others' needs and confident of God's provision are those best engaged in God's purposes. Such heart motivation has always been the fuel that is supposed to drive God's people in their provision for his worship. God said to those he had released from slavery in Egypt, "From every man whose heart moves him you shall receive the contribution [for the tabernacle] for me" (Ex. 25:2; cf. 35:5).

The apostle Paul has given us the ultimate standard: "Each one must give as he has decided in his heart, not reluctantly or under compulsion, for God loves a cheerful giver" (2 Cor. 9:7). God does not want us to be controlled by a formula or by fear but rather to be freed up for generosity by the cheerfulness that results from confidence in God's gracious eternal provision.

5

Success

I READ AN ARTICLE RECENTLY about Joseph Dear, once the chief investment officer for the nation's largest pension organization. The person who interviewed Dear said, "We expected dry, sculpted responses from such a high official of such a large fund, but Dear surprised us. He was as funny as he was wise. He was as humble as he was brilliant. He was our favorite interview."[1]

If you're the chief investment officer of the wealthiest pension fund in the world's wealthiest nation, then how do you measure success? The interviewer didn't just celebrate Dear's wealth. He also celebrated his wisdom and humor and the fact that he gave a good interview. Yet despite those measures of success, it was the interviewer's final comment that made me reflect on the nature of true success: "Joseph Dear was diagnosed with cancer soon after our interview. He passed away yesterday."

Malcolm Forbes reportedly said many years ago, "Whoever dies with the most toys wins." If that were the true measure of success, then Joseph Dear would be a winner. But I doubt if many people really believe that statement. What I am certain of is this: whoever dies with the most toys dies. And none of the toys or money will go with that person. As one person quipped, "There are no Brinks trucks in a funeral procession."

In this chapter I want us to focus on the question, How do we measure success as believers? Whether you're in business, education, or any other endeavor, you can't measure success unless you have a goal.

What's the goal you're trying to achieve? That will define your view of success. Most people would say that the mark of success in corporate business is when you maximize shareholder value. In academics, it's raising student achievement. In art, it's long-term recognition. But if your goal is to bear Christ's name in the workplace, as well as into the world, then you recognize that the measure of your success is how well you have magnified the name of Jesus.

In Deuteronomy 8, Moses explains to the Israelites how they should view the promised land that God is giving them. His explanation also helps us to understand the meaning of success in the twenty-first century:

The LORD your God is bringing you into a good land, a land of brooks of water, of fountains and springs, flowing out in the valleys and hills, a land of wheat and barley, of vines and fig trees and pomegranates, a land of olive trees and honey, a land in which you will eat bread without scarcity, in which you will lack nothing, a land whose stones are iron, and out of whose hills you can dig copper. And you shall eat and be full, and you shall bless the LORD your God for the good land he has given you. (vv. 7–10)

According to Moses, what it means for God's people to be successful is to make a good life from the resources God gives, and then to "bless the LORD" (v. 10) for all that he provides.

Honoring God through Our Gifts

We tend to think of blessing as something we receive. But when we bless God, it's something we give. We give God honor. We give him glory. When we make good use of the resources God puts into our lives, we're blessing him by honoring his purposes.

By contrast, when we fail to use God's gifts according to his priorities, we dishonor him and rob him of blessing. What that means is we must measure success in our own lives by asking, "How have I used the gifts, talents, and resources God has put in my life to honor him?"

When gifted musicians make music, that honors God.

When farmers diligently prepare their harvest, that honors God.

When businesspeople maximize shareholder value according to biblical priorities, that honors God.

When engineers move earth or open the skies to our travel, endeavor, health, or understanding, that honors God.

When teachers share information, and most particularly when they brighten futures, that honors God.

When parents nurture the gifts of their children, that honors God.

In Ephesians 2:10 Paul writes, "We are [God's] workmanship, created in Christ Jesus for good works, which God prepared beforehand, that we should walk in them." As we use the gifts God has given us, we are fulfilling his mission and his purposes—and blessing God!

Multiplying Our Gifts

But we don't bless God best by merely using gifts. He expects us to maximize the gifts that he has given and multiply the blessings they provide. Deuteronomy 8:12–13 describes a time when the people of Israel will "have eaten and are full and have built good houses and live in them, and when [their] herds and flocks multiply and [their] silver and gold is multiplied and all that [they] have is multiplied." By using God's gifts and resources in obedience to his will, God's people were to experience a multiplication of his blessings. So also, we properly use the gifts of God by employing them in ways that multiply his blessings.

In the parable of the talents in Matthew 25:14–30, Jesus talks about a master who gives to his servants several talents—five to one, two to another, one to another—and then leaves on a journey. When the master returns, he discovers that the one who had received five talents had made five talents more, and the master says, "Well done, good and faithful servant." Likewise, when the master learns that the one who had received two talents had made two more, he says, "Well done, good and faithful servant." Clearly, the master believes that the total amount is not as important as the effort to multiply his provision. The only servant who does not receive praise from the master is the one who was given one talent. Instead of investing and multiplying that talent, he buried it. He failed to make good use of what the master had given him and received a rebuke.

The parable of the talents is really a wonderful message of God's grace. God doesn't measure our value by whether we have many talents or just one. His level of care is not determined by whether we are rich or have modest means. His favor is not determined by whether we do white- or blue-collar work. The Lord does not value us for our accumulation; he simply gives us the responsibility of using the resources he provides to multiply his blessings. When we so bless his purposes, that's biblical success.

In Tim Keller's book *Every Good Endeavor*, he talks about an estate planner who wondered, *How does my job of helping people disperse their wealth after they're dead honor God?* At that time, he was helping a Christian woman who wanted to bless Christ's mission with her resources after she passed on. She had an eternal perspective for what could be done with what God had provided during her life. Her perspective enabled the estate planner to realize that his work had an eternal dimension that could make it an act of worship.[2]

I have read other accounts recently of people who are using the resources God provides, in the opportunities God provides, for the purposes he designs.

Bethany Jenkins, who has worked for The Gospel Coalition, described a bus driver in Alabama who had been on the same route for seventeen years. During that time, the bus driver had touched over three hundred students because she realized that her job was her opportunity to witness and show the hand and heart of Christ day after day. One of the students was a special-needs girl who was often agitated when she got on the bus. The bus driver noticed that the young woman was agitated on the days that her father's car was in the driveway, and the bus driver began to suspect that things were not right. She reported the situation to the authorities, and as a result she changed the future of that child. The bus driver was not wealthy or famous, but she took the resources God had given her and used them for God's purposes. And that was success.

There is a wise and respected cardiologist in my congregation named Don McRaven. Many in our community owe their lives to his wisdom and skills. Now, because of his age, Dr. McRaven is more often in the hospital as a patient instead of caring for patients. When our minister of pastoral care visits him, the minister sings with his guitar. That's to be expected. But to the surprise of patients and staff alike, the respected doctor also joins in the songs. Like Paul and Silas in prison long ago, the minister and the doctor belt out hymns that echo down the hallway so other patients can hear of God's abiding love. Dr. McRaven can no longer practice medicine, but he can still sing. So he uses the voice that God provides to care for patients. He is still using God's resources in God's opportunities according to God's design.

It does not matter how young or old you are. What matters is that you are faithfully doing what God is calling you to do. That's the ultimate mark of success—not fat paychecks or professional accolades but using God's resources in God's opportunities for God's design. That's what blesses the Lord and his people.

Freedom through Obedience

In our culture, some people believe that their purpose in life is to experience "the freedom of being me." But often that kind of "freedom" is merely sanctified selfishness that excuses the worst of this world's evils. In the name of freedom, people abandon their marriages, ignore others' needs, exhaust resources on passing thrills or personal indulgence, give in to sexual immorality, and become totally self-centered under the banner of "I'm free to be me."

That's why Moses says in Deuteronomy 8:11, "Take care lest you forget the LORD your God by not keeping his commandments and his rules and his statutes, which I command you today." Moses is speaking to God's people, who have recently been released from slavery, reminding them that the way to experience true freedom from everything in the world that would threaten to enslave them is to follow God's commands.

Why does he say that? Because when we follow God's commands, we are preserved from spiritual harm by walking the good and secure path of God's provision. In 8:14–16, the Lord tells the Israelites:

> [I am] the LORD your God, who brought you out of the land of Egypt, out of the house of slavery, who led you through the great and terrifying wilderness, with its fiery serpents and scorpions and thirsty ground where there was no water, who brought you water out of the flinty rock, who fed you in the wilderness with manna that your fathers did not know, that he might humble you and test you, to do you good in the end.

The words remind Israel and us that we should follow God's ways because he has our best interests in mind. He is the one who takes his people out of slavery. And when we try to throw off the shackles of God's standards, we don't become free. We reenter slavery.

Think of Bernie Madoff who got rich by abandoning all standards of ethics to cheat investors. He not only wound up in prison but impoverished his family and hundreds of others. His jail was made not simply of steel and concrete but of guilt, shame, and regret for selfishness that ultimately blessed no one.

Or remember Johnny Manziel, the Cleveland Browns quarterback who had tremendous talents and abilities. Yet through partying and alcohol he made a wreck of his life. A lifetime of shameful regret in the shadows of the life "that could have been" is his perpetual ball and chain. Through such examples and the grace of his word, the Lord is telling us, "I've got something better for you. Just as I delivered Israel from slavery, I'm also trying to protect you from becoming enslaved by practices or patterns that will deprive you of the blessings I intend for your life."

Enslaved by Expectations

If faithfulness to God is not our measure of success, then the world's expectations will become our standard. Our culture tells us that success is measured by owning a big home, driving a luxury car, wearing nice clothes, bossing many people, or having enough money to take a recreational rocket trip to space. If we're defining success by what we accumulate or achieve, we become driven by the desire to show people we're successful. Then whatever segment of culture we're trying to impress plays the tune that we're going to dance to.

If you're an artist, your mark of success may be personal recognition. If you're an athlete, it may be your number of wins or how many records you set. If you're a builder or realtor, success may be measured by your reputation, how many contracts you have signed, or how many sales you have made this week, this month, or this year.

When we meet other people's expectations in these ways, we feel good for a while. But if we fail to meet or maintain those expectations, then we feel like a failure or begin to fear we will fall from the summit of our success. We begin looking for the next deal or recognition that will prove our continuing significance.

As a consequence, we become a slave to others' expectations, as well as our own ambitions.

God wants to deliver us from that kind of slavery and to provide everything we need to experience his blessing in our lives.

I suppose there's not been a much better example of someone experiencing personal success without knowing God's blessing than Cam Newton before and after the 2016 Super Bowl. Prior to the game, his mother sent him a lengthy text that said: "Cam, you have a big platform. Represent the awesome God you serve through your words. . . . Speak boldly to the nations that you represent Christ for the great things he has done in your life. Through your language and actions, speak words to uplift. . . . Remember your God."[3]

Pretty good advice, Mom! That was well said. But after Cam lost the game, his hoodie was up, his head was down, and during the press conference he offered single-word explanations for the game's outcome, ultimately walking out of the interview. When he was challenged that he should be a better loser, he responded by saying, "Show me a good loser and I'll show you a loser."

Here was a man with tremendous talents, a tremendous future, and tremendous accomplishments. Yet his assessment of himself was "I'm a loser." Why? It was because he did not meet his personal expectations or those of other people.

What if he had been able to recall what his mom said? She had said, "Remember God." When he was so embarrassed in that interview, what if he'd been able to say, "Folks, the game did not go the way I wanted. But my identity is in Christ. I am united to the King of the universe who gave his Son to die for me. I am eternally treasured. All of this will pass, but I will be with my Savior forever, and he loves me no less because I fumbled a football."

In the worst moments of our lives, when we are shocked by what people have done or said—things that affect our reputation, our job, or our family—we need to be able to say, "My identity is in Christ. I am held dear by the Creator. He treasures me." That affirmation can free us from other people's expectations, so that we can live in faithfulness to the one who has been faithful to us—and measures our success only by how we use his resources and our opportunities (even the opportunities of trials and afflictions) to bless him.

God's Unconditional Love

How do we respond then, when we know that faithfulness is the mark of Christian success, and yet we have not succeeded in our faithfulness? At such times, we need to remember what God said to Moses and the people of Israel in Deuteronomy 8:17–18:

> Beware lest you say in your heart, "My power and the might of my hand have gotten me this wealth." You shall remember the LORD your God, for it is he who gives you power to get wealth, that he may confirm his covenant that he swore to your fathers, as it is this day.

We stand before God because of what he has done for us, not because of what we have done for him. He provides the resources that enable us to succeed. God also establishes the covenant love that provides those resources and maintains his care when we do not deserve them.

Such covenant love is based on his promises rather than our performance and culminates in the provision of Jesus Christ.

Through him we learn God will never say, "If you do good, then I will love you." Instead, he says unconditionally, "I will love you, pardon you, and provide for you. Now live for me with the resources I supply in the opportunities I develop for the blessings I will multiply for eternal good."

As Christians, we are most blessed when we remember that it is God's power that has provided for us to bless him and fulfill his purposes. Such power is never of our making, but it is ours to employ for the blessings God intends. We make the best use of God's power and resources by remembering the old gospel message:

> Not what my hands have done
> Can save my guilty soul;
> Not what my toiling flesh has borne
> Can make my spirit whole. . . .
> Thy work alone, O Christ,
> Can ease this weight of sin;
> Thy blood alone, O Lamb of God,
> Can give me peace within.[4]

His provision came first. His mercy came first. So even when we fail in our faithfulness, we remember that God called us, and his covenant keeps us always. We can come to him again, saying: "God, forgive me and heal me and help me, not because of my faithfulness but because of yours."

God is always faithful to answer that prayer! This is our solid foundation for success, no matter what life brings or the world thinks. We can be successful because God is faithful. And because God is faithful, we are successful whenever our lives bless him.

6

Humility

IN RESEARCHING THE CLASSIC business book *Good to Great*, Jim Collins discovered that only eleven out of 1,435 companies he studied achieved greatness, which he defined as superior stock returns over fifteen years after a major transition at a company.[1] What defined those eleven companies was what he called a "Level 5 leader," someone who has a paradoxical blend of personal humility and a fierce determination to promote the good of a company over personal interests.

In our day, a leader is often viewed as an almost super-human visionary who ascends to the mountaintop and then begins to play business and people like chess pieces on a board, resulting in outstanding success and profit. In contrast, Jim Collins describes a Level 5 leader as someone who "demonstrates a compelling modesty, shunning public adulation and never boastful. . . . Demonstrates an unwavering resolve to do whatever must be done to produce the best long-term results, no matter how difficult. . . . Yet on the other hand . . . [c]hannels ambition into the organization and its work, not the self, setting up successors for even greater success in the next generation."[2]

For those of us who are students of the biblical teaching on humility, we want to cheer and say, "See, I told you the Bible was right! Here is the proof. Even secular research affirms that nice guys do *not* finish last and that ruthlessness is *not* the path to success. The values of Scripture are the best path to succeed even in the business world."

That sounds so great!

But there are a couple of problems.

While Jim Collins does describe the value of true humility, he never explains how you get it. Nor does he ever establish how you can guarantee the results of humility. After all, even if you are a Level 5 leader, you may not be able to transcend an economy that goes bust or a product that is out of date or people who are truly evil.

Humility is not a business plan. It is a quality of character that is built in the heart for a type of personal success not able to be quantified in profit-and-loss models. That's why we need Jesus to teach us about humility, in Matthew 21:1–17:

Now when they drew near to Jerusalem and came to Bethphage, to the Mount of Olives, then Jesus sent two disciples, saying to them, "Go into the village in front of you, and immediately you will find a donkey tied, and a colt with her. Untie them and bring them to me. If anyone says anything to you, you shall say, 'The Lord needs them,' and he will send them at once." This took place to fulfill what was spoken by the prophet, saying,

"Say to the daughter of Zion,

'Behold, your king is coming to you,
  humble, and mounted on a donkey,
  on a colt, the foal of a beast of burden.'"

The disciples went and did as Jesus had directed them. They brought the donkey and the colt and put on them their cloaks, and he sat on them. Most of the crowd spread their cloaks on the road, and others cut branches from the trees and spread them on the road. And the crowds that went before him and that followed him were shouting, "Hosanna to the Son of David! Blessed is he who comes in the name of the Lord! Hosanna in the highest!" And when he entered Jerusalem, the whole city was stirred up, saying, "Who is this?" And the crowds said, "This is the prophet Jesus, from Nazareth of Galilee."

And Jesus entered the temple and drove out all who sold and bought in the temple, and he overturned the tables of the money-changers and the seats of those who sold pigeons. He said to them, "It is written, 'My house shall be called a house of prayer,' but you make it a den of robbers."

And the blind and the lame came to him in the temple, and he healed them. But when the chief priests and the scribes saw the wonderful things that he did, and the children crying out in the temple, "Hosanna to the Son of David!" they were indignant, and they said to him, "Do you hear what these are saying?" And Jesus said to them, "Yes; have you never read,

"'Out of the mouth of infants and nursing babies
  you have prepared praise'?"

And leaving them, he went out of the city to Bethany and lodged there.

Matthew 21 stands in stark contrast to a typical depiction of a triumphant conqueror we know from the movies: The king comes home on his battle steed. The trumpets blare. The people cheer. The king salutes the troops. They raise their swords. Then servants roll out a red carpet woven from rare cloth and golden threads for the king to ascend his throne.

In contrast, King Jesus is a lowly carpenter who rides on a donkey, not a war horse. The crowds who gather are not ranks of royalty but the kind of common people who always flock to Jesus. They put down palm branches because they cannot afford rare cloth. They lay down their clothes because no one owns a carpet. He ascends to a cross before assuming his throne. What kind of king is this? This is a king who chooses humility as his badge of honor.

A closer look at Matthew 21 will tell us that true humility is never forced on us by either people or circumstances. It is a matter of choice. Humility says, "For the sake of a greater purpose, I choose to forgo my personal interests." We see Jesus repeatedly making that choice in this chapter despite who he is and the amazing claims made about him.

Jesus Is a Prophet

Matthew shows that Jesus has the authority of a prophet because he both makes prophecies and fulfills them at the same time. In Matthew 21:2–3 Jesus says to his disciples, "Go into the village in front of you, and immediately you will find a donkey tied, and a colt with her. Untie them and bring them to me. If anyone says anything to you, you shall say, 'The Lord needs them,' and he will send them at once." Jesus knows that there is a donkey tied with a colt, he knows what the conversation will be, and he knows that the one who owns the donkey will agree to let it go with his disciples. In other words, he's able to prophesy, to see into the future.

Beyond that, he recognizes that his own ministry is the fulfillment of prophecy. The same chapter tells us that Jesus's words about the donkey were "to fulfill what was spoken by the prophet, saying, 'Say to the daughter of Zion, "Behold, your king is coming to you, humble, and mounted on a donkey, on a colt, the foal of a beast of burden"'" (vv. 4–5).

This prophecy was first given in the book of Zechariah five hundred years before this moment of fulfillment in Matthew's account. Zechariah lived during the time of King Darius, the ruler who threw Daniel into the lions' den. Yet despite his immediate trials, Zechariah assures God's people of God's ultimate goodness by telling them that a king is coming—a humble king who will ride on a donkey, bringing salvation with him. This king is not like Darius, who throws people into lions' dens. He will save them from the evil lion, Satan himself.

Zechariah's prophecy is being fulfilled by Jesus as he rides into Jerusalem on the donkey. That's why the crowds can say that "this is the prophet Jesus, from Nazareth of Galilee" (Matt. 21:11).

Jesus Is a Priest

Matthew tells us that Jesus is not only a prophet but also a priest. He fulfills that role by going to the temple in Jerusalem and purifying it.

He overthrows the tables of the money changers and the chairs of those who are selling animals for sacrifices. Then in verse 13 he tells these profiteers, "It is written, 'My house shall be called a house of prayer,' but you make it a den of robbers."

Matthew tells us that the outcasts—the blind and the lame— come to Jesus in the temple, and he heals them. The chief priests and the scribes see the wonderful things that Jesus is doing, but they refuse to praise God, and they rebuke children when they cry out in praise. In contrast, Jesus receives the children's praises.

As a priest, Jesus declares judgment upon those in the temple who are self-righteous, but he accepts the outcasts and defenseless who acknowledge his care.

Jesus Is a King

Of course, the major claim that is being made in Matthew 21 is that Jesus is Israel's long-anticipated king. Look again at verse 9: "The crowds that went before him and that followed him were shouting, 'Hosanna to the Son of David! Blessed is he who comes in the name of the Lord! Hosanna in the highest!'"

Each word or phrase that Matthew uses clearly identifies who Jesus really is. *Hosanna* is a combination of two ancient Hebrew words, *hoshia na*, which could be translated as "save us." If the word *hoshia* sounds familiar, it's because it shares the same root behind Jesus's own name, *Yeshua*. Even though the people don't fully understand what they are saying, by crying out "Hosanna," they are saying, "Save us, Jesus."

The people also call Jesus the "Son of David," the long-prophesied messiah from the line of David who will have both an eternal and universal kingdom. To confirm that their king has come, many put their robes on the ground before him. Their actions call to mind what was said and done for a previous Israelite king named Jehu in 2 Kings 9:12–13. There we read, "'Thus says the LORD, I anoint you king over Israel.' Then in haste every man of them took his garment and put it under him on the bare steps, and they blew the trumpet and proclaimed, 'Jehu is king.'"

Matthew tells us that others in the crowd cut down branches and laid them in the path of Jesus. These actions echo events surrounding an earlier Jewish revolt against the Greek ruler Antiochus Epiphanes. He was a cruel leader who defiled the temple in Jerusalem by putting a pig upon the altar and ordered the Jews to worship Zeus as the supreme god. History also describes these actions of Antiochus:

> He ordered his soldiers to cut down without mercy those whom they met and to slay those who took refuge in their houses. There was a massacre of young and old, a killing of women and children, a slaughter of virgins and infants. In the space of three days, eighty thousand were lost, forty thousand meeting a violent death, and the same number being sold into slavery. (2 Macc. 5:11–14)

The actions of Antiochus Epiphanes were so terrible that the apostle John uses him as the archetype of the antichrist in the book of Revelation.

When Jewish liberators overthrew Antiochus Epiphanes, and God's long-oppressed people wanted to celebrate their victory, they had no red carpet to unroll. So they cut branches from the trees and put them down in the roadway as if to say, "This is the only carpet we can offer to those who have saved us."

As Jesus is coming into Jerusalem, the people also cry out, "Hosanna in the highest!" Normally, the Jews used this expression only once a year at the Feast of Tabernacles. This feast celebrated the fact that God dwelt in his tabernacle among the people of Israel during their time in the wilderness and provided for their daily sustenance. During each of the seven days of the feast, the people declared God's deliverance by saying, "Hosanna." But on the eighth day, they circled the altar of provision seven times and then declared, "Hosanna in the highest," as if to say, "Now we invite the high hosts of heaven as well as the people of earth to praise the king who comes to save us."

The prophet is here.

The priest is here.

But more than anything, the King is here.

Hosanna in the highest!

Humility and Courage

Prophet, Priest, and King Jesus rides a donkey on a path covered with clothes and palm branches, because no one has provided anything more appropriate.

When we recognize that the King of the universe demonstrated that kind of humility for our deliverance from personal sin and a corrupted world, we must begin to ask, "What would such humility look like in our world—whether we labor in an office, worksite, or at home?"

What would it mean to put aside the bonus that we deserve so that someone else could keep their job? Or to give up a promotion requiring a move so that our family could be held together? Or to submit to a decision requiring personal sacrifice without sulking?

We can only demonstrate such humility to those around us by trusting God to work through us and our circumstances, accepting dishonor, disrespect, or disadvantage without resorting to bitterness or despair. Instead we submit our priorities to God's purposes with the intention of bringing honor to him and his salvation to others.

Humility of this sort should not be confused with timidity. Matthew tells us that Jesus demonstrates not only humility but also great courage. He enters Jerusalem and heads to the temple. Then he overthrows the tables of the money changers and the chairs of those who are selling the sacrifices. As a consequence, we read, "The whole city was stirred up" (21:10).

Roman documents tell us that as many as 250,000 lambs were being sold at this time for the Passover sacrifices in Jerusalem. Because of the pressure that the slaughter of 250,000 lambs would put on sanitation and facilities, the priests had a rule: every lamb must cover at least ten people. If there were 250,000 lambs, there could have been as many as two and a half million people coming into Jerusalem.

Imagine these people going up the huge, stone steps of the great temple in Jerusalem, hundreds of thousands ascending to offer their sacrifices. They are purchasing lambs for sacrifice. They are buying pigeons if they can't afford the lambs. To pay for these sacrifices they must use money that comes from other currencies because, at Passover, these Jews come from many different nations in pilgrimage. Consequently, there's profit to be made in their money exchanges.

Imagine what is going to happen if Jesus upsets all this. There are stakeholders whose profits are at risk. Passover sales for the businesspeople of ancient Israel are like our retail profits for Christmas, Easter, and the Fourth of July all in one week.

Jesus is upsetting the whole system. He's not just upsetting the business. There are people who come from all over the world and think, "If I offer this sacrifice and am good enough, I'll be okay with God." They are depending on their good deeds to gain God's favor. In contrast, Jesus is saying through his actions, "I am disrupting not only your business but also your superstitious use of God's temple. You can't buy his pardon."

Both unfair profit and false beliefs are being challenged here. Jesus knows the risk that he is taking by challenging these practices and beliefs to ensure the integrity of the gospel. But he submits his interests to his Father's purposes. That's true humility, not timidity.

Because Jesus is a prophet, he also knows what's going to happen to him after he overthrows the money changers and those who profit from selling animals for sacrifice. Matthew 20:17–19 tells us:

> As Jesus was going up to Jerusalem, he took the twelve disciples aside, and on the way he said to them, "See, we are going up to Jerusalem. And the Son of Man will be delivered over to the chief priests and scribes, and they will condemn him to death and deliver him over to the Gentiles to be mocked and flogged and crucified, and he will be raised on the third day."

He knew what was coming. Yet he kept coming.

The apostle Paul tells us that Jesus was willing to put aside his heavenly glory for the people he came to save: "Though he was in the form of God, [he] did not count equality with God a thing to be grasped, but emptied himself, by taking the form of a servant, being born in the likeness of men. And being found in human form, he humbled himself by becoming obedient to the point of death, even death on a cross" (Phil. 2:6–8). Jesus knew the costs, counted the costs, and kept his appointment with God's plan for his passion. Great courage was required for such humility.

What does that kind of courage look like in our places of work? It looks like standing for what is right when we know it will cost us. Or, as another writer has said, it requires that we "be willing to show up for the suffering."[3]

Humility and Determination

When Luke describes what Jesus was willing to do, he says, "When the days drew near for him to be taken up, he set his face to go to Jerusalem" (Luke 9:51). He was not going to be diverted. He was not going to change his course in any way that would lessen his impact on his mission.

One of Jim Collins's keys to success is called the "Hedgehog Concept," by which he means having a single unrelenting purpose.[4] But if we follow Jesus's example, having a single purpose can lead us not only to worldly success but also to suffering that succeeds in fulfilling God's purposes.

What does that look like in our world today? What does it mean to risk the deal to preserve integrity? To endure the scorn to oppose what is unethical? To be undeterred by ridicule for righteousness' sake? To say for the sake of Christ and those who witness our lives, "I will show up for the suffering?" What does such humility look like? It looks like courage clothed in selfless determination; like self-sacrifice robed in the glory of God's Son.

One of the privileges I have had in my life is being able to rub shoulders with Christian businesspeople who own or run significant companies. Many of these people are donors to the seminary I led, and I praise God for them. I watched some of them during the great recession of 2008 as they made difficult decisions for the survival of their companies. Two could have received great personal wealth if they had sold their companies to larger corporations that were using the down economy to pick up smaller businesses at a bargain price. Yet my friends refused to sell their companies because they knew that many of their employees would lose their jobs through the consolidations the deal would demand.

These business owners were willing to forgo their own wealth for the good of their employees' future and families. In short, these leaders showed up for the suffering, and their example taught me that God's greatest glories shine through those with the determination to put others' interests above their own. God can do amazing things through those whose honor reflects Christ's humility.

The culinary arts world was shocked not long ago when Matthew Secich, one of the nation's super chefs in Washington, DC, gave up his prestigious position in that city's most well-known restaurant and set up a deli in rural Maine. Why did he do it? He explained, "As a Christian, I had grown disgusted with the relentless pursuit of the four-star rating, the earned reputation, and customers and profits and fame that drove me to tyranny with my employees. In order to get the four stars, I burned people."

That became literal one night when one of the line chefs messed up an order. To punish him, Secich held that line chef's hand over an open flame. That event sobered Secich, not only from the pursuit of fame but also from relying on Jim Beam to medicate him from the pressure he felt every day. He wrote, "I went home and in humility got down on my knees and asked forgiveness from the God who had humbled himself on the cross."[5]

Matthew Secich's testimony went around the world in the news media because he was willing to say, "I'm going to show up for the suffering. I'm going to sacrifice glory for the sake of the testimony of Jesus and the people he loves."

Humility and Love

We cannot understand the humility of Jesus if we only visualize him with a carpenter's strength and a king's rage purifying the temple. We must also look closely to see the love in his eyes. We all can identify with some aspects of the relentless pursuit for fame, for approval, for people to say we're doing great. A drivenness to accomplish what is needed to be acclaimed by the world is not rare. Yet Jesus tells us, "Even if you do not have the acclaim of the world, I have loved you with an everlasting love, and you are mine forever."

We perceive this compassion in our Savior when we remember Jesus's specific words as he drove the money changers from the temple: "It is written, 'My house shall be called a house of prayer,' but you make it a den of robbers" (Matt. 21:13). The first part of the statement is from the Old Testament prophet Isaiah. God said through the ancient prophet, "My house shall be called a house of prayer" (Isa. 56:7), and Jesus quoted those words when he cleansed the temple.

But Isaiah says a bit more than the Gospel of Mark records Jesus paraphrasing: "My house shall be called a house of prayer *for all peoples*" (Isa. 56:7; cf. Mark 11:17). The house of prayer that God established and that Jesus cleansed was not only for Israel. It wasn't just for the Jewish people. It was to be a house of prayer for *all* people.

Jesus quotes Isaiah to display the wideness of our God's heart. Long ago God used a prophet as he now uses his Son to say, "My house should be the place where people gather from every nation to experience my compassion. In this place, you should pray that people throughout the world will come to know my grace."

Jesus's heart is stirred because he is driven by his Father's compassion. That compassion made him willing to endure mockery, ridicule, scourging, and ultimately the agony of the cross. He humbled himself before all that so that we could experience God's forgiveness and receive eternal life through him.

Now he calls us to follow his example by humbling ourselves for the sake of others. The Great Commission will never be fulfilled by those straining for personal recognition, driven by pride, and focused on their own gain or glory. The gospel can only be honestly proclaimed by those who humble themselves, selflessly expressing the courage, determination, and compassion that is needed to make plain the gospel priorities of a Savior who would put the needs of others above his own interests—who would die to self so that others might live.

7

Glory

A HEADLINE IN THE *Chicago Tribune* newspaper captured an unlikely glory: "City Tries to Pump Up Its Crews Down Under." The article described a pep rally for eight hundred employees of the Chicago sewer department. The new head of the department was seeking to rouse his workers to enthusiasm for a tough and dirty job. He shouted in his speech, "Winning is not a sometimes thing; it's an all-time thing!" Then a photo accompanying the story showed a huge banner on the wall behind him announcing the goal of this winning attitude: "Bringing Sewers Above Ground."[1]

Whether *that* is a goal we would endorse is not as important as noting the zeal that resulted from giving glory to it. When sewer employees believed that their dirty and smelly work would not be hidden underground but shown as crucial for a huge city to function, they had enthusiasm for their work.

God also intends to give us zeal for our work—whether it be dirty, difficult, or mere drudgery—because it brings glory to him. Of course, simply saying that our jobs can bring glory to God doesn't make it obvious how this can really be true. There is often a disconnect between what we perceive as God's glory and many of our tasks. Even the most celebrated jobs have their sewer features. No one likes cleaning up messes, doing inventory, calming volatile bosses, filling out expense reports, or addressing angry constituents. How can such jobs bring God glory? The answer is not so much in the nature of the job but in the purpose of the person who does it.

Made for Glory

Already we have seen how God designed humanity to bear his likeness (chapter 1). The opening pages of the Bible tell us:

> So God created man in his own image,
>   in the image of God he created him;
>   male and female he created them. (Gen. 1:27)

Men and women were made to mirror the character and care of God—to reflect his glory. The ancients call this aspect of our being the *imago Dei* (the image of God) in us.

Of course, we do not bear God's image perfectly. We can be like a child in a photo, pushing a toy mower behind his dad's mega-horsepower lawn tractor. Like the child, we reflect our Father's image imperfectly, but the reflection is still unmistakable. We can get so hung up on how poorly we fulfill God's purposes that we miss the importance of being an "image bearer" for God and the enthusiasm for our work that springs from this distinction.

When God declared that he would make humanity in his image, he said, "Let them have dominion over the fish of the sea and over the birds of the heavens and over the livestock and over all the earth and over every creeping thing that creeps on the earth" (Gen. 1:26). Humanity was to use the animals and resources of sea, sky, and soil to flourish and reproduce, but not simply for personal gain. Earthly resources could never be used selfishly, recklessly, or thanklessly if humanity were to fulfill its purpose of mirroring God. To be an image bearer of God, humanity would have to reflect God's compassion for all that he had made (Ps. 145:9).

In Adam and Eve's initial context they were to "keep" the garden of Eden by caring for it. Their calling was to steward the resources of the garden so that it would flourish. But God's image-bearing purposes for humanity were not limited to that first garden. God blessed the first man and woman by saying to them, "Be fruitful and multiply *and fill the earth*" (Gen. 1:28). At one level, we can read this verse as blessing the intimate union of a man and woman that produces children. At another level, it is a revelation of the wider purposes for which the Lord made us.

Those who are made in God's image are to "fill the earth." We are to take the features of his glory to every place we inhabit and to every job we do. As we express his character and care, our work pushes back the darkness of a fallen world and brings the glory of God to light. By necessity, such work often begins where the drains and sewers of a broken creation run deep. But as we take God's image into that darkness or dreariness, his glory shines more and more in that place. The consequence is that work of every sort and in every place can glorify God if our purpose is to extend his character and care even to the grimmest and grimiest of situations.

Our work is not so much ennobled by the tasks we do or the skills we exercise, as by the purpose God accomplishes through us. The nineteenth-century poet Gerard Manley Hopkins explained, "To lift up hands in prayer gives God glory, but a man with a dungfork in his hand or a woman with a slop pail gives him glory, too. He is so great that all things give him glory *if you mean that they should*."[2]

Meaning Glory

By intending to reflect God's image in our tasks and skills, we are extending his glory more and more widely into our fallen world, until the knowledge of his glory covers the earth as waters cover the sea (Hab. 2:14). We were made for glory, and the regard we or others may have for our job doesn't change or limit that purpose. In fact, often the glory of God is most on display where his people are most dedicated to displaying his goodness and grace in difficult or demeaning contexts.

One of the largest churches in our nation was founded by Pastor Frank Barker. Honesty would compel you to acknowledge that he was not a great orator, but people flocked to his church because of his willingness to go anywhere and do anything that would bring glory to God.

Once he showed up on a Saturday morning to help a neighbor wash his car. He also showed up for the next *eight* Saturday mornings to help with the same lowly job. When the neighbor finally asked, "Why are you doing this, Frank?" the suds-soaked pastor replied, "Because I don't think you are a Christian, Don, and I am looking for the opportunity to explain Christ to you."

Frank is now beyond his pastoral ministry years, but the neighbor remains a faithful leader in the church because of a pastor who knew any task can bring glory to God so long as we mean that it should.

The sixteenth-century Reformer Martin Luther made it plain that God's purpose ennobles any task by writing, "When a father goes ahead and washes diapers or performs other menial tasks for his child in Christian faith, God, with all his angels and creatures, is smiling, not because that father is washing diapers, but because he is doing so in Christian faith."[3]

In faith we trust that God has planted his image in us to be taken to the workplace and that the tasks we do are made glorious not primarily because of the glory in them but because of God's purpose for us.

God is present in our work no matter how shabby or sudsy it is because those made in his image are doing it. We bring him to the workplace. We display him in our work. We serve him in our tasks by bearing his image in the darkest, stinkiest, dullest endeavors. In each of these, Christ displays himself through our character and care.

We may readily see how God gets glory when the football hero points skyward after a touchdown or the Nobel laureate acknowledges her faith, but the reality is that most work in the world is highly repetitive, pressured by deadlines, bone-wearying, and mind-numbing. Yet the one who represents Christ in the boardroom or the assembly line with integrity—who speaks to the thousandth complaining patient or customer with Christlike care, or who endures insult and isolation to polish the image of God for those who have not known or experienced his grace— spreads God's glory. This is the purpose for which we were made.

Making Glory

As image bearers of our Creator, we are to reflect God's glory, but we are also to reproduce it. God's glory becomes real and apparent to others by the way our labors extend his rule and reputation. As our products and practices honor God, more and more people are able to experience the effects of his character and care.

Of course, we cannot actually manufacture the glory of an infinitely powerful, holy, and wise God. That is above the pay grade of every imperfect human. Still, we are to work in such a way that those who work with us, and those who are served by our work, see and experience more of God's love for all that he has made (Ps. 145:17).

Ancient church fathers called this aspect of our work that makes God's priorities and purposes apparent to the world our "labor with God" (*labore cum Deo*). The designation echoes the apostle Paul's description of our role in spreading the message of Jesus: "We are God's fellow [or co-] workers" (1 Cor. 3:9).

Paul was speaking of being a fellow worker with God in ministry and mission work, but the "coworker" concept of our everyday labor is not limited to work that produces explicitly Christian messages or is deliberately evangelistic. Rather, we are always to be working with God to make his glory touch every aspect of our world because we carry his image into every job we do. With that perspective all work is ministry and mission.

Of course, we would and should run from any job description that simply reads, "manufacture God's glory," as if human efforts could create divine splendor. But what if God were to say, "Glorify me," and then add, "Fear not, for I am with you; be not dismayed, for I am your God; I will strengthen you, I will help you, I will uphold you with my righteous right hand"? We don't have to guess if God will offer such support. This is precisely what the prophet Isaiah tells us God promises (Isa. 41:10). The same God who promises never to leave or forsake us promises to help us fulfill the purposes for which he made us in every circumstance and task (Heb. 13:5).

Through Christ's provision, our heavenly Father sends the Holy Spirit to be our helper so that we can spread the glory of God. The Spirit gives us knowledge of God's will in his word, the resolve to do as he instructs, the strength to carry it out, and the promise to make our work more worthwhile than we can ask or even imagine. So whatever we do, we do it all for the glory of God (1 Cor. 10:31).

This may sound simple: we are to bring glory to God in whatever we do, and God will be with us to help us do it. But what precisely is it that God wants us to do to make more glory for him?

Loving Glory

When God gives that first job description in Genesis to "fill the earth," he adds, "and subdue it" (Gen. 1:28). Earlier we saw that this mandate to take control of the earth's resources for God's purposes can never be understood as sanctioning selfish, reckless, or abusive uses of God's creation. But earth's resources are to be used for something. What is it?

Christ Jesus helps us understand when he answers the question, "What is the greatest commandment?" He answers, "You shall love the Lord your God with all your heart and with all your soul and with all your mind. This is the great and first commandment" (Matt. 22:37–38).

We are to love God with all our resources. He is the priority of our attitudes and efforts. When we use the earth's resources, we are to use them in ways that honor the Lord and show our love for him. Perhaps that makes most sense when we think of the things that we do in worship. Our words and music and gathering places should show our love for the Lord. Actions and attitudes honor the one we love.

Of course, our love should not be limited to our times of worship, so we also honor God in our homes, our play, and our work. By doing what is just, compassionate, and good, we obey the commandment to love God. But what do actions and attitudes that are just, compassionate, and good look like outside of our places of worship? Jesus answers that question with the second greatest commandment, which he says is like the first: "You shall love your neighbor as yourself" (22:39). So the commandment to love God with all our resources takes shape in everyday life by loving our neighbors as much and as well as we love ourselves. This means that the work that brings God glory is also the work that demonstrates his and our love for our neighbor.

What does neighbor love have to do with our work? Pastor-scholar Dan Doriani demonstrates with an account that is painfully candid in its characterization of the struggle many Christians experience when thinking about how to bring glory to God at work. Doriani writes:

> Lisa and Ryan both have honest jobs, but their church cannot seem to discuss work in ways that help them. The pastor affirms that all work matters to God, but his illustrations tend toward clearly *productive* vocations: doctors, teachers, engineers, and farmers. . . . [He says] faithful Christians work hard, operate with moral integrity, support their family, and give generously if they prosper. These are good points. Indeed, it is good to be productive and to resist the temptation to moral compromise. But there is more to fidelity in the workplace. . . .

Many people have trouble seeing the value of their work. In truth, work is the chief place where we love our neighbor as ourselves. . . . At work we have the greatest capacity to care for the hungry, the thirsty, and the sick. If, by faith, we consecrate our work to God and love our neighbors, clients, and customers, he [God] will remember it forever.[4]

Two remarkable things are said in this passage: our work is the chief place where we can love our neighbors, and such love has an eternal impact. How could either be true?

Describing four transportation workers who struggled to see the value of their work, Doriani explains how work expresses love for neighbor:

Where would consumers be without the trains and trucks that distribute food? Will they drive themselves to Kansas to buy a cow, to Idaho for potatoes, to Minnesota for wheat? If we reflect, we realize that everyone in the chain of production contributes to the food supply. . . . Suppliers sell seeds, fertilizer, targeted herbicides, and equipment, while farmers till the ground, plant seeds, and harvest the crops. . . . After the harvest, food processors, packagers, truck drivers, stock boys, and cashiers have their role. . . .

God gives everyone a role as well as a place of service. We pray, "Give us this day our daily bread," and God call farmers, truck drivers, and cashiers to collaborate to bring us bread. . . . We tend to think that we feed the hungry when we volunteer in a soup kitchen, but that is shortsighted. . . . At work we have the greatest capability to meet legitimate human needs.

If, by faith, we consecrate our work to God and aim to love both our co-workers and our customers, we serve the Lord and he remembers it.[5]

It may help us to assess the way in which our labor provides love for our neighbor by again applying the "George Bailey test" reflected in the classic Christmas movie *It's a Wonderful Life*. The awkward angel in George Bailey's life gives him the privilege of seeing what others' lives would have been like had he not lived. The privilege, of course, leaves George begging to live the life he almost sacrificed.

We can consider our work in similar ways: Had there not been farmers or real estate agents or computer engineers or chemical manufacturers, how would life be different for customers, employees, their families, their neighbors, or their communities?

If you think about it carefully, we all make a living doing things that someone believes are necessary for others' lives to flourish. That's why our work is the chief place that we show love to neighbor. By our work others live, love, raise families, discover beauty, have fun, find dignity, and discover the necessity of God's work to make it all work together.

The apostle Paul writes, "We are his [God's] workmanship, created in Christ Jesus for good works, which God prepared beforehand, that we should walk in them" (Eph. 2:10). Every deed and duty of our work is a link in an eternal chain of God's purpose that he designed for us to do before the world began. So our work has eternal significance, and the Bible promises that God will remember our faithfulness to his plan—and to the neighbor we love by serving him (Ps. 112:6).

This is not to say that every job is glamorous according to the world's standards. Earlier I mentioned that I'd observed a worker on an assembly line whose entire job was making sure that packages of cheese slices sealed properly. He watched thousands of packages pass by him every hour on a conveyor belt, sorting out those improperly sealed. I thank the Lord that is not my job, but I have no right to demean the job itself. I have no way of knowing how suited the worker was in intellect and temperament for the job. Yet, I know for sure that his attention to his quality-control tasks protected consumers, kept the company's reputation and coworkers' salaries secure, and provided income for his family as well as many others.

Valuing Varieties of Glory

Our jobs do not have to be essentially the same to be equally valuable for God's purposes. When Jesus tells the parable of the workers in the vineyard (Matt. 20), each laborer receives equal pay for work that varies greatly in the time invested and the work accomplished. Christ's purpose was to undermine the currency of any economy that estimates human value simply by the nature of comparative performance.

Those who win a 100-meter dash in less than ten seconds and those who win a marathon running more than two hours can claim the same gold medal. Each is recognized for doing what they were designed and appointed to do. Whether we fulfill God's purposes by doing what brings earthly acclaim or enduring what fulfills heaven's ends, we further God's glory and bring the good he intends for our neighbor.

The world may not recognize the significance of our labors, but believers have the assurance that our jobs matter to God and make a difference in the lives of those he loves. Because we are image bearers of our Lord, our labor brings God to our workplace and sends his blessing into the world touched by our work. Christ is present in us as we work, he is present with us as we work, and he is made present to others by our work. In such ways, all of us work with as much divine purpose as preachers and priests in the world's finest churches.

Priests of Glory

Modern writers Matthew Kaemingk and Cory Willson bring fresh insight to the ancient concept of the "priesthood of believers" when they write, "All work, when done in faithful service to both God and neighbor, is a priestly act of worship. . . . When workers enter the sanctuary, they don't arrive for a moment of worship; they've been engaged in priestly worship all week long."[6]

I expect the idea of everyone who works being a priest will seem foreign or foolish to most people. Who can imagine that the daily tasks of writing emails, sweeping floors, delivering meals, drafting contracts, driving trucks, collecting fines, driving to soccer games, selling shoes, teaching class, giving therapy, leading companies, etc., are priestly duties? Yet, if we see our workplace as the location where we display and dispense God's glory, we may begin to realize that it is our daily parish and then may be prepared to consider our priestly role.

In the workplace we don't wear priestly robes, but we are clothed with Christ (Gal. 3:27). We don't lift our hands in prayer, but we do pray for God to bless our labors and our fellow laborers. We don't deliver sermons, but we do express the character and care of Jesus in what we do and how we do it.

We don't administer sacraments to sinners, but we do distribute the blessings of our faith despite the pressure of bosses or the pettiness of coworkers. We don't offer counsel in confidential chambers, but we do offer the patience, instruction, and compassion of Christ as we deal with the unruly, discouraged, arrogant, and ambitious.

Most workers are not in ordained ministry, but all are responsible for extending the boundaries of the kingdom of God by practices and products that enable his transformation of our world according to his priorities. We pray, preach, and minister Christ's care by working with priestly intent.

In ancient times the nature of the sacraments offered in worship may have made the priestly connection of workers more apparent. On the Communion table in front of them laborers could see the blessings of Christ being offered in elements they had produced. The bread and wine were from ground they had tilled, grain they had ground, grapes they had crushed, dough they had kneaded, and ovens they had stoked. The work of priests and workers was interwoven in making God's glory and grace known.

Still, the instinctive divide between the sacred and secular tends to keep all of us from considering our role in God's redemptive work. An account from the time of Gregory the Great tells of a woman who walked forward to receive the sacrament from her priest. As she received the bread, the priest said to her, "This is Christ's body broken for you," to which the woman responded in laughter. When asked why, she explained that what the priest called "Christ's body" had just come out of her own mixing bowl and oven a few hours earlier. It seemed absurd that work so recently from her hands could be the means of Christ presenting himself to his people.[7]

The spontaneous laughter of the candid baker is no doubt echoed in the minds of many who think it absurd that they should be called to make Christ present to others as his priests in their workplace. Yet when we view our ordinary labor as the means by which God is doing his extraordinary work, the blessings of our labors multiply with the extension of his glory.

A friend of mine manufactures adhesive products. The business has been quite successful—so successful that larger competitors have consistently sought to take over or cripple his company with nuisance lawsuits. Because my friend is a Christian, he seeks to work ethically and contribute generously to his church with the profits of his business. For much of the life of his company, he has seen these responsibilities as his primary ways of honoring God through his work. That perspective has made him wonder why the Lord has not taken away the pressures of his competitors to enable him to give more to kingdom purposes. The wondering has led to some deep discouragement.

Only recently has my friend begun to see things differently. He still believes that the Lord wants him to operate ethically and to give generously, but he has also begun to consider how his products (and not just his profits) can be integral to God's kingdom purposes. Helping his perspective were a series of severe hurricanes across the southeastern United States. The hurricanes not only created a vast new market for adhesive products that could help windows resist wind, but they also more directly revealed to my friend how his business could be an expression of God's glory. The adhesive products were saving thousands of homes and businesses and relieving suffering for tens of thousands of families and communities. From that perspective, the quality and quantity of adhesive products were distributing the care of God. In addition, my friend's commitment to fair practices (such as not price gouging when it would have been easy to take advantage of storm crises) displayed the character of God.

My friend no longer sees his business only as a means to provide for his witness inside his company and his generosity toward his church. He sees the development and production of his products as a way of glorifying God by using the knowledge, resources, and opportunities to extend the kingdom priorities of security, compassion, and peace—what theologians call *shalom* (the peace that God's rule over all brings).

Not only has there been a renewed sense of purpose in this Christian businessman's operation of his company, but there has also been a liberating new perspective on the nuisance lawsuits that have so discouraged him. Rather than simply questioning why God has not allowed him to give more to his church through a business unencumbered by legal challenges, my friend has begun to see his business as a powerful instrument for extending God's glory.

With that perspective, he has an explanation for why there have been such great challenges to his success: Satan only bothers to attack those who threaten him. So the business challenges have become strange affirmation of how significant Satan must believe are the kingdom blessings God is bringing through *adhesives* intended to glorify him.

Yes, sometimes my friend still gets discouraged and wishes the challenges would go away. But he knows that in this fallen world no one gets a pass on trouble until Christ returns. So my friend labors on with the priestly intention of making much of God's glory through products manufactured according to God's priorities and for his kingdom's purposes.

Multiplying Glory

The perspective that honest work of all kinds can bring glory to God has wonderful precedent in the way God instructed his covenant people to honor him.

When the Lord had delivered his people from slavery in Egypt and established them in the promised land, God instructed them to bring the firstfruits (not the late crops or the leftovers) of their labor to his altar (Deut. 26). Those whose occupations involved livestock instead of crops were similarly instructed to bring their firstlings (the firstborn animals in their herds) to God's altar.

Throughout the ages, believers have continued to honor God in ways that echo this ancient instruction. Not only do football players point skyward after a touchdown, but cattle herders, shepherds, farmers, orchard keepers, and gardeners habitually lift the firstfruits of God's blessing skyward in recognition of God's provision of herds and harvests. Parents similarly instruct their children to put their first pennies from a lemonade stand in the church offering, and adults in new careers honor God with a portion of the first paycheck.

Such offerings may make little difference in the economies of the world, yet they signify each worker's gratitude for God's present provision as well as the trust that he will continue to provide. So common are these gestures of worship among believers that it is striking that the original act of worship on which these habits are based was not intended only to affirm faith or even thanksgiving. The Lord's instruction included these words, "And you shall rejoice in all the good that the LORD your God has given to you and to your house, you, and the Levite, and the sojourner who *is among you*" (Deut. 26:11).

The devotion of the worker that provided food portions for the ancient priests caused rejoicing for those whose profession was leading worship for God's covenant people, but it was also to stir rejoicing in those who were not covenant people. Sojourners (travelers from other nations) too were made witnesses of God's glory by the offering provided from each profession.

The offerings were each worker's testimony that the goods and services that made life possible were ultimately from God's hand. Human labor would never have been sufficient for sustenance or worship had not God provided soil, seed, and seasons that our hands cannot. So, the offering was a testimony to the grace of God's provision that served as a witness to both the covenant people and to those still searching for the true God.

God's intention to use the firstfruits and firstlings of vastly different professions to honor him among the faithful and the foreign demonstrates a startling dimension of his intentions for our occupations. They are all intended to glorify him and multiply others' awareness of his grace.

Mission of Glory

Every day that we go to work with the willingness to acknowledge that our products and profits are ultimately from God's hand, we are participating in God's mission to multiply those who will acknowledge his glory. Not only missionaries and preachers, but all who labor with the intention to honor God through their business, skills, sweat, politics, creativity, and conduct are participating in the mission of God (*missio Dei*).

God does not call all Christians to leave their profession to become missionaries, but he does give all Christians a missionary calling in their profession. Work and witness are intertwined in God's purpose of taking his glory to every corner, closet, community, company, and nation of the world. All people in all professions are the object of his mission, and as we work among them, we are at work for him in the task of multiplying those who recognize, profess, and participate in his glory.

This is not the way that we tend to think about our "secular" professions, but it is the way that God has designed his world and called his people to be his ambassadors in every aspect of it. The fact that we have not previously considered how our job aligns with God's mission does not mean that we should not consider it now.

Twentieth-century theologian Lesslie Newbigin wrote, "We need to create, above all, possibilities in every congregation for laypeople to seek illumination from the gospel for their daily secular duty. . . . The work of scientists, economists, political philosophers, artists and others illuminated by insights derived from rigorous theological thinking."[8]

It may seem foolish to expect believers in every profession to engage in "rigorous theological thinking," but such reflection is actually the path of relief and rescue from the daily grind that can seem without meaning or significance. No one who works honestly is doing nothing (1 Cor. 15:58). God has placed his people in the professions and places he intends in order to multiply those who can witness the realities and necessities of his grace. Each believer's occupation and tasks are significant not because they receive the recognition and reward of the world but because we engage in them with a divine commission to glorify God through them.

By product and conduct we are on God's mission in our workplace, helping to transform little or large ecosystems in our assigned sector of God's world according to his eternal plan. Further, by acknowledging that any blessing we experience is ultimately from his hand, we offer to God our thanks, and we offer to our neighbors, workmates, and supervisors witness to his grace.

God commissions believers in many different occupations to fulfill his sovereign plan of extending his kingdom's influence and multiplying those who will gather around his throne in eternity to sing the praises of his goodness. The multiplication may not occur in our awareness or in our lifetime, but it will occur.

When Jesus characterizes the judgment that will culminate our existence in this world, he does not say that every believer will have done things of great earthly significance, even in their own estimation. Still, he will say to each of them, "Come, you who are blessed by my Father, inherit the kingdom prepared for you from the foundation of the world. For I was hungry and you gave me food, I was thirsty and you gave me drink, I was a stranger and you welcomed me" (Matt. 25:34–35).

Curiously, those so recognized do not recall doing what Jesus commends. They ask, "Lord, when did we see you hungry and feed you, or thirsty and give you drink? And when did we see you a stranger and welcome you?" He responds, "Truly, I say to you, as you did it to one of the least of these my brothers, you did it to me" (25:37–40).

The message is that a deed is counted great in heaven not because of the impression it makes on the one who does it or on others who may or may not notice it. Our work is made significant by the one who is served by it. When our labors serve him, they are made glorious because they fulfill the commission that fits into his eternal purposes.

Those purposes are made plain by the full story of Scripture. From its beginning, the Bible tells us that we were made in God's image to reflect his glory wherever we go and whatever we do throughout the world. At the end of the Bible, we learn how far his glory has spread as a consequence of our labors. The apostle John describes the scene that commences our future existence in heaven's glory:

> I looked, and behold, a great multitude that no one could number, from every nation, from all tribes and peoples and languages, standing before the throne and before the Lamb, clothed in white robes, with palm branches in their hands, and crying out with a loud voice, "Salvation belongs to our God who sits on the throne, and to the Lamb!" (Rev. 7:9–10)

The glory God sovereignly planned for our world he graciously completes through the lives and labors of those he commissions to fulfill his mission. Such a mission is not completed simply by the preaching of able pastors and the sacrifice of noble missionaries. It is completed by the eternal work of God through the daily work of our lives.

In the mundane and in the magnificent, in the significant and the insufferable, in the skilled work and in the "good tries," in the successes and in the honest failures, God is expressing and extending his glory through faithful believers that honor his name in the work they do.

Perspectives for Glory

The winners of the 2021 National Public Radio Student Podcast challenge were eighth graders from the Sayer Middle School in Lexington, Kentucky. Their unlikely subject for achieving such glory was their school's maintenance staff. One of the young students explained: "We talked with lots of people about our maintenance staff and what they do every day . . . *so we can do what we come here for.*"

That perspective gives nobility to the mopping of halls, the servicing of furnaces, the unclogging of toilets, and the host of "lowly" duties that enable a community's children to learn, advance, and prepare for careers that will also enable them to support their families, advance the common good, and secure a future in which many more can flourish. With a similar perspective:

- Battery researchers and manufacturers believe they are solving fuel issues and saving the planet.

- Politicians believe they are advancing justice, national security, and a prosperous future for our nation.

- Salespersons believe they are taking care of their families and contributing to our economy because no business can prosper until somebody sells something.

- Doctors see beyond the pressures and repetitiveness of clinical practice to the lives, families, and communities made healthy by their labors.

- Highway workers understand that without their labors, every trip becomes dangerous, the nation comes to a halt, the economy collapses, and our suffering becomes universal.

- Preschoolers' moms are not simply changing diapers, building Lego sets, and enduring exhausting days, but are shaping the joy, health, and faith of little bodies inhabited by eternal souls.

- And, yes, to return to the cliché of an old tale, the bricklayer can believe that he is not merely stacking bricks, but building cathedrals and homes for future generations, and research centers for vaccine discoveries, and police stations for the safety of neighborhoods, and art museums for the preservation of beauty.

Such perspective is not merely a cliché but the teaching of Scripture for those with the hearts to receive it. God ennobles every task and occupation by making each integral to the flourishing of his world and his people.

The ways we honestly and conscientiously do our work, as well as our willingness to witness to coworkers, bring God glory, but so does the work itself. By our labors, our communities thrive, lives are vitalized, earth's resources are stewarded for good, families are blessed, cultures advance, and faith is made possible and available for all whose lives flourish through the touch of God's grace dispensed by those working "as for the Lord and not for men" (Col. 3:23).

By such work others see our good deeds and are made able to give glory to our Father in heaven (Matt. 5:16).

8

Evil

I KNOW THAT THIS WILL BE the most difficult chapter I write for this book. The concepts are not difficult, but they force us to face truths that deeply trouble all workers. I lead us down this path so that we are not mistaken about the glory that work offers. Yes, there is much good that God intends to accomplish through our labors, but there is much evil in the working world that resists his intentions and opposes the good we want to accomplish.

The apostle Peter warns all who seek to glorify God with the strength he provides, "Do not be surprised at the fiery trial when it comes upon you to test you, as though something strange were happening to you" (1 Pet. 4:12). Nothing previously said about magnifying and multiplying the glory of God through our work is untrue. Still, we are not prepared for the dignity or difficulty of our work if we do not recognize how God's glory and our good will be opposed in a fallen world.

The Evil of the Fall

In the opening chapters of the Bible, all God's promises to redeem our world and work are given in the context of a world that resists the advance of God's kingdom with weeds and thorns, weakness and blame, deception and death. God gave to our first parents a sure hope that one would come from their progeny who would crush the influence of Satan in our world. We praise God for that first gospel promise of Christ's victory over evil. Still, we must not forget that woven into that prophetic hope was an ominous warning: Satan will strike the heel of the Savior (Gen. 3:15).

While Satan would ultimately be crushed, he could still wound. And until he is utterly vanquished by Christ's eternal kingdom, the evil one intends to wound those who bear the image of the one who will crush him by their work in this world.

What does that wounding look like? All who work know. It looks like working for a boss who demeans or with coworkers who ridicule, or being leapfrogged in a promotion by someone operating unethically, or taking heat from a customer who is wrong, or losing a job because of another's lie, or facing the unending pressure of trying to keep a company going in a failing economy or amidst changing technology.

Satan wounds when God's people lose their jobs for doing the right thing. Satan wounds when Internet trolls flame those doing their best or, by contrast, defend fellow slanderers to destroy the reputations of good people. Satan wounds when those doing secular work forget their spiritual values and when those doing spiritual work adopt secular priorities to succeed.

We need to be clear, however, that the wounding we now experience in the workplace is not solely due to present evil intentions or wrongdoing. God cursed the ground after the sin of our first parents to show us the consequences of turning from him on earth and to turn us to dependence upon him for eternity. So, much of the wounding we now experience is a consequence of working in a world that experiences the brokenness caused by Satan's influence over many centuries.

The original glory of God's creation will not be restored until Christ's return. That means not all of the difficulty we experience is due to supervisors, coworkers, and competitors making evil choices. The weeds and thorns of God's curse upon creation that invade contemporary workspaces are all the complexities and complications of a world that abandoned God's rule long ago.

Expected Evil

Without the order and blessing that controlled God's original creation, the work that many of us do for a season of life or for the sake of others does not seem glorious at all—it seems miserable. Though we are right to discuss how God's mission can bring nobility and purpose to our work, we are wrong to ignore the deep sadness and even humiliation many experience while working in a fallen world. The true glory of many jobs is being faithful to God in them, despite the misery of them.

The evil of a fallen world can make everyday work degrading, stressful, ugly, unhealthy, unfair, oppressive, mind-numbingly repetitive, morally compromising, and soul-sickening. Praise God if your job is rewarding, meaningful, intellectually challenging, and spiritually edifying, but realize this is not the work that most people do in this fallen world.

Often, even the jobs for which we qualify with advanced degrees and multiple promotions become routine or dissatisfying after years at the same tasks. We climb to the top of the ladder of success and find it is leaning against the wrong building. Business executives and medical professionals tired of board meetings, yet another strategic plan, and consumer complaints look wistfully at artisans, farmers, and teachers, wondering if a meaningful life was wasted chasing a buck.

Other chapters in this book are intended to help believers see ways of glorifying God in the difficult and demeaning jobs we may have to do for the sake of family care and personal survival, but this chapter echoes warnings of the apostle Peter that could be summarized like this: "Don't be surprised if your job is enduring your job with the strength Jesus gives" (see 1 Pet. 2:20 and 4:11–16).

Being forewarned is being forearmed. We will not be prepared for the trials and tasks of this life if we adopt the modern view of Christianity that presumes God promises his people upward mobility and easy living.[1] Jesus called his followers to take up a cross daily (Matt. 16:24) and not to be surprised that the evil of this world will result in many trials for those who bear his image (John 16:33).

The most common experience of believers in most cultures is job security that provides daily bread—and not much more. Some Christians also experience the blessings of financial or professional success that give them particular obligations for generosity according to God's purposes. Still, none of us will be prepared for the challenges that inevitably come to fallen creatures in a fallen world if we do not recognize there will be times that God calls each of us to face evil in ways that may jeopardize success, financial security, and even daily bread.

Accepted Evil

As international economics began to devastate the farming and mining industries of a community where I once pastored, rescue seemed to come in the form of a large printing company that employed thousands. But as competition threatened that industry too, the company found security in printing what reputable companies avoided: pornography.

So from every small town and church in that region, the company employed everyday people in this everyday work that everyone accepted with the explanation that times were hard and families had to be fed. God wouldn't expect otherwise, would he? The answer to that question was plain to those outside the community but not to those who were facing the loss of employment, family security, and the entire region's economic lifeblood. Not until the area's pastors banded together, jeopardizing their positions, did key lay leaders in the churches take an even more courageous stand.

Despite attacks from coworkers and family members, the lay leaders acted on the conviction that the eternal souls of their families were more important than their earthly sustenance. Believing that the evil was real and that God had called them to resist it, these leaders risked everything dear to them on earth by stepping off the production line whenever the pornography was produced.

Those outside the community may think that they would have made better, or different, or quicker choices. It's easy to judge the actions of others when *you* have nothing to lose. But for those who were risking their family's welfare and continuance in a community where they had lived, farmed, or mined for generations, the steps toward crushing Satan's influence were the steps toward their cross in their workplace. Those steps were taken only because evil was assessed for the spiritual threat it truly was, and resisting evil was assumed as the biblical responsibility it truly is.

Eventually, international competition, changing technology, and Internet pornography shut down the printing company. By then the churches had taken their stand, faithful Christians had mostly retired or left the company, and, thankfully, their children were secure in other locations or industries because their parents had steered them in more godly paths. The community continues to struggle economically, but the courageous steps of God's workers that had jeopardized earthly security became God's means to secure eternity for those who loved him and bore the glory of the cross in the face of evil.

The Evil of Others

Jesus was honest and clear about the evil in the world that would threaten those who would follow him: "'A servant is not greater than his master.' If they persecuted me, they will also persecute you" (John 15:20). That evil can come in many forms and from those we would not expect if we did not have Jesus's warning.

Writing about the African-American experience in the worship settings of the post–Civil War South, James Cone writes:

After being told six days of the week that they were nothing by the rulers of white society, on the Sabbath, the first day of the week, black people went to church to experience another definition of their humanity. . . . When blacks went to church . . . they realized that [Jesus] had bestowed a meaning upon their lives that could not be taken away by white folks. . . . That affirmation enabled black people to meet "the Man" on Monday morning.[2]

Those who originally taught these black people that they were made in God's image and loved by the Savior were the preachers of the enslavers and sometimes the enslavers themselves. At work, masters denied the humanity and the divine image-bearing of the slave; at worship, they were forced to affirm both, however inadequately or inconsistently.

Looking for consistency in sinners is, of course, a vain enterprise, whether they call themselves Christian or not. Instead, all Christians should be prepared by the example of the African-American experience for the evil that parades as care or security, knowing that evil in the form of oppression, harassment, false values, and idolatrous temptations can come from the very ones we count upon to provide our security.

When our historic church building aged beyond reasonable repair, the people stretched beyond their means to construct a wonderful new facility. True to their biblical priorities the new building not only provided beautiful worship space but also facilities to serve and reach our community with Christ's heart.

The contractor had built other churches and affirmed our values, and we rejoiced to see the foundation laid and the walls rise. Then the wiring and plumbing began to go in, requiring a visit from the city's fire inspector. He quickly informed us that the building would not meet the local construction code and would require massive and expensive adjustment.

Our building committee immediately contacted the contractor to find out how such terrible errors could have been made. The contractor's response astounded us. "Oh," he said, "when you told me what you wanted and how much you wanted to spend, I did not think that you wanted to meet building codes. There are ways around such things. Don't you have a city councilman on your board of deacons?"

The man was clever but his message was clear: if you want your building at this price, find a way around the safety codes, even if that means improperly influencing city officials. Don't worry about ethics, or safety, or witness. Just get the job done.

Decades later the choice we made seems clear and easy. We went back to our congregation, presented the problem, faced the anger and blame of some, and raised more money from the faithful to do the job the right and safe way. Yet at the time, the uncertainties and pressures were so massive (could our people provide for the added expense, would they support leaders who had gotten them in this mess, would they continue with the pastor who had led them down this path?) that the contractor's suggestions were powerfully enticing.

The man we trusted to build and secure our worship was the very one who most tempted us to abandon our principles and jeopardize our church's witness and families' welfare. I praise God that the church's leaders ultimately saw the contractor's suggestions for the evil they were and chose another path. I also praise God that his people were willing to walk that path. But I cannot promise that the story will always turn out so rosy.

The Trials of Evil

This remains a fallen world, and evil can have its day, even if God will have the final say. Until then, we will constantly face deception, dishonesty, disloyalty, and difficulty—often from those with whom we work.

Our tendency is to think the evil that confronts us is because of some error or weakness in us. Indeed, it may be, but it is also true that much of what the world considers our faults or failures are the consequences of evil we did not cause and may not be able to counter in this life. Pastors, business people, professionals, parents, educators, and artisans all need to understand that "fiery trials" are par for the course in the Christian life until Christ returns.

So what is plain for now is that those who stand for Christ will need to stand against evil. Jesus said that was inevitable. What is also plain is that having to face career obstacles or occupation trials is not necessarily an indicator that a Christian has done something wrong or that God has failed. Faithful Christians will face persecution, trial, and tragedy because we live in a fallen world and because evil will wound. If that happened to Jesus, it may well happen to us who want to walk his paths.

Because evil is present and real throughout our world, our jobs not only give us obligation and opportunity to resist evil, but they are also a consistent weapon in Satan's arsenal to attack us spiritually. Perhaps it seems strange to say that the occupations that are designed to magnify and multiply God's glory are also a means for Satan to extend evil into our lives, but we know this is true.

Deforming Evil

All persons' jobs have the opportunity to form and deform their spiritual solidarity with the Savior.[3] By resisting evil, promoting kingdom purposes, striving for Christ-honoring relationships, and exhibiting godly character, the Holy Spirit is forming us into followers of Jesus who are more Christlike in habit and heart. In contrast, when we yield to the evils of the workplace, the deformities from God's design more and more characterize us.

Because evil is real and pervasive in our fallen world, we need to recognize that these deformities are frequently the result of the twisted relationship we have with our work as a consequence of the fall. The work that God created for our good and his glory can be hijacked by the priorities of others and, if we are not on guard against the subtleties of such evil, we can be seduced by them.

The joy that we should take in working hard and stewarding the gifts and skills that God has provided to us can be twisted into ambitions that create workaholics that have lost touch with their families, God's rest, or life's beauty.

The good work that we should be zealous to do so that we can bring glory to God and provision to our families can become selfish pride or a means of trying to satisfy an approval addiction.

The energy and smarts that are God's gracious gifts become merely the means to compete with, beat, and move past others so that patience is perceived as weakness, compassion as marketing, and tenderness as waste.

The income and provision we receive for productivity and creativity shift from being causes to praise God for his care to being the bases for comparisons that either feed our sense of self-importance or gnaw at our gut with coveting the possessions of others who have more.

My job as a Christian leader raising funds for institutions and churches has frequently put me in the context of some of the world's richest persons. Early in such ministry I learned the dictum of all fundraisers who will stay sane: "Thou shalt not covet the lifestyle of your donors." When meeting with the wealthy, it's easy to fall into the trap of wondering why God has not been equally as good to someone "as good as me." This is especially true when you discover the frequent character flaws of those who hold the wealth that is the lifeblood of many Christian organizations.

Three things have helped me: (1) witnessing the humility of the truly rich, who believe that God has blessed them to enable them to support his work; (2) discovering that those made wealthy for God's purposes have responsibilities for his kingdom's care and maintenance of their wealth that others could not bear, or else God would have given them similar wealth; and (3) remembering that no matter how wealthy the persons in our society, they will spend 95 percent of their time at home between the bedroom, the refrigerator, and the digital screen—and so do I.

Even many we think of as poor in the United States live in relative affluence compared to those in much of the rest of the world and through the scope of history. Still, that's hard to remember when everyone in your office or organization is competing for position, recognition, and income.

When we let others set the standards for what will make us happy, then the provisions God is making for our care easily become the idols of our hearts. Stephen Smith explains with revealing and painful candor:

What I am going to tell you here has been scraped out of the hearts of thousands of leaders I have worked with in my life—men and women who are leaders either in the marketplace or in some sphere of Christian ministry. These good people hit a dead end somewhere in their journey. Some have made mistakes. Some have left carnage behind them. . . . I have witnessed much despair as leaders try to climb the slippery, treacherous slope of success. The reality is that they're at the bottom, and it feels like hell. In fact, it hurts like hell.

Here I will confess that I was one of those who lost their way. I swallowed the pill that promised success. I drank the liquor of my profession for many years and became intoxicated with my leadership. . . . Life for me was about my work. It became a mistress who promised me everything but in the end delivered nothing.[4]

Key to understanding all that Smith is saying is the note that those who worked with such warped drivenness were "good people," often "in some sphere of Christian ministry" who were still capable of "mistakes" in their lives and "carnage" in the lives of others.

The Evil of the Good

We can all understand how evil can triumph in the form of unethical behavior, unfair promotions, oppressive supervision, blind ambition, heartless profiteering, and dishonest business practices. What we struggle to acknowledge is that all of these can—and usually do—come from "good people."

I have led Christian organizations for most of my adult life. In those settings, I have been stolen from, lied to, falsely accused, threatened, forced out of organizations and off boards, betrayed by those I trusted, abandoned by friends, blamed for the misdeeds of the ones doing the blaming, and . . . the list could go on.

I have also watched fear make friends run from their duty, jealousy make colleagues turn from their principles, lust destroy trusted leaders' marriages, longing for significance turn godly allies into cheap slanderers, and ambition turn gentle shepherds into plotting wolves willing to sacrifice organizations, friends, and their own families for personal promotion.

As I make these lists and bring to mind the persons involved, two things occur to me: (1) I cannot think of a single instance in which the ones doing such evil were not professing Christians; and (2) I imagine that anyone reading the lists could reasonably conclude that I must be a terrible leader to head organizations so broken. After all, if I were doing everything right, wouldn't people be inspired to live in God-honoring ways? Wouldn't good management result in good outcomes? The simple answer is, not necessarily, but we will not be prepared to answer that way without a good theology of evil. Here is one key aspect of that theology: "No one is good except God alone" (Mark 10:18). Jesus said that, but it flies in the face of the theology that I want to believe.

I want to believe that good people will not be overcome by evil, that their faults and fears and prejudices will not get the best of them. I want to believe that if I just manage well and treat people fairly and offer enough encouragement and set a good enough example, the Lord will always grant success. That's my gut under-standing of how the work world should work. So when a company boots out a leader, when a church vomits out a pastor, when a board rejects its chairman, when an organization rebels against a long-term chief, or when a company fails, I presume the leader was incompetent or did something wrong.

What I do not put into this instinctive equation, until I have experienced such rejection or failure myself, is evil. My inadequacies can certainly be one explanation for my organizations' and employees' struggles, but not the only possible explanation. The Bible carefully reminds us of the complex nature of God's people and the greater challenges his leaders may face with biblical biographies that counter simplistic reasoning about success and failure.

By the time of Israel's rebellion in the book of Numbers, Moses has led the covenant people for four decades. He has led them out of slavery, through the Red Sea, across the wilderness, and against multiple enemies in numerous battles. For the sake of his people, he has sacrificed royal position, defended the helpless, shared leadership, shown courage, and walked humbly with God.

He has also pleaded with God for the lives of idolators and worked with God to punish idolatry. He has delivered the law that will guide God's people in good and safe paths. He has set up a tabernacle to atone for sin when people wander from the law. His prayers have provided manna for the hungry and meat for grumblers. His obedience has brought water to rebels from a rock in the desert.

Yet despite his exemplary leadership, Moses himself attests that his people "assembled themselves together against Moses and against Aaron. And the people quarreled with Moses" (Num. 20:2–3). Previously, they had threatened to kill him for their wilderness woes, even after he had rescued them from Pharoah (Num. 14). Numerous times the people considered replacing Moses, turning to gods other than his, or turning back to Egypt.

Yet more discouraging than all of these acts of rebellion and rejection was their frequent source. The ones who turned from Moses were not just the rabble and renegades, but trusted leaders and his own family—his wife, his brother, his sister. Each in turn doubted him, questioned him, and tried to turn others from Moses or to turn Moses from God.

It's certainly possible that Moses could have been a better leader, but the emphasis of these Scripture passages falls not on his leadership failings but on exemplary leadership that faced evil in others with faithful perseverance. In present situations also, it's certainly possible that organizational crises can be due to leadership failings, but the realities of a fallen world also mean that leaders and organizations will face evil and the challenges of a fallen world that are not of the leaders' making nor due to their faults.

The Ends of Evil

The Lord may use lesser challenges of evil (including those that seem to be terrible setbacks) to prepare leaders for greater challenges to come. Christian leaders' greatest challenges are frequently in their senior years. This is counterintuitive. We tend to think that seasoned leaders will have gained the expertise to guide their organizations through challenges so that their later years will be the most productive and easy. Frequently the opposite is true.

Often the most capable and experienced leaders face their greatest challenges at the pinnacle of their careers where the rewards of success *and* the possibilities of failure are greatest. Despite personal ability and experience, the realities of a fallen world are always ready to teach us that there are forces of economy, humanity, and evil that are more than a match for any person's wisdom and skills.

Leaders that I highly respect in business and ministry have often been surprised not only that their greatest challenges came in their later years, but also with the frequent source of the challenges. These Christian leaders were caught off guard because, despite their theology of evil, their years of experience had convinced them that they had all the puzzle pieces of organizational leadership in place to succeed in their final ventures. They thought they knew what to expect and how to handle it.

The unlikely source of evil that came so late, so aggressively, and so unexpectedly was good people whose pettiness, jealousy, ambition, or greed took over for a time. Good leadership cannot prevent all the crises of life and challenges of evil. Such leadership responds with faithful obedience and trusts God to provide what is best for the organization (and its leadership) in his time and in his way. This does not mean that all evil can be overcome by our skills or without our suffering. Some defeats, disappointments, and pains are not avoidable in a broken world. Jesus went to the cross. Not all good leadership is marked by success or even survival.

The Evil in Me

What makes it possible to bear the evil of our world and the betrayal of others? Two things: confession of the commonness of evil and confidence in God's faithfulness.

When we have suffered from evil, we can be tempted to many more evils. We may, of course, excuse ourselves of all wrongdoing and blame others for our hurts and failures. There may be sound reason for this. But even if there is, nursing such perspectives and wallowing in our pain can lead to other temptations of isolation, doubt, despair, hardness of heart, and unwillingness to trust others or to serve God again.

When we have been betrayed, wounded, and embarrassed by our losses, we naturally seek shelter. A time of healing may very well be needed, but permanently sealing our hearts away from deep relationships does not allow us to employ the gifts and graces we steward for Christ's sake. Even if we are never able to work again with the income and prestige of the job that wounded us, there are hurting souls in the world that need our experience, care, and understanding of God's grace. If all we do is descend into self-absorbed pain and perpetual licking of our wounds, then we will inevitably doubt God's providence and distort his care.

Never does human suffering deny the goodness of God or the usefulness of his servants. The prophets, apostles, and people who did God's will in Scripture often suffered great loss due to this world's evil. Moses was betrayed by his people, David by his friends and family, Paul by his fellow travelers, and Jesus by his apostles. The most idealized father in Scripture (who represents God himself) was disrespected by both of his sons (Luke 15:11–32). Few of us would be so bold as to sidle up to any of these biblical figures and say, "Now, if you had just been a better leader, manager, or servant of God, then these terrible things would not have happened."

Neither the experience of failure nor the duplicity of those we trusted proves that we failed to do what God desired or that the Lord has no further purpose for us (Ps. 41:9). A. W. Tozer wrote, "It is doubtful whether God can bless a man greatly until he has hurt him deeply."[5] Such hurt forces us from dependence upon our fallible strengths and unfounded pride to the holy acknowledgment that apart from Christ we can do nothing (see John 15:5). In that confession is the true source of spiritual strength for God's calling upon our lives.

The Antidote to Evil

God's calling through the trials of evil can be fulfilled only by our spiritual union with Christ. It cannot be fulfilled if our hearts are full of rage and bitterness or are cold and distrusting. While deep hurt may make us appropriately wise and wary about human relationships, if we cannot love and trust again, then we cannot rediscover joy or reflect Jesus.

Our trials and crises teach us to depend upon him alone through whom all things are yet possible (Phil. 4:13). The reason the Scriptures tell us not to put our "trust in princes" or a "familiar friend" is that evil resides in every heart, and all are capable of betrayal, abandonment, and selfishness (Ps. 55:13; 146:3). We must not make an idol of any job, person, or position by making such the source of our joy or the guarantor of God's love.

This does not mean we are never again to believe or cherish others. Despite the pain of our pasts, we remain called to appreciate and participate in the redeeming work that God is doing in others' lives. Our children still need our tenderness, our neighbors still need to see Christ in us, and our enemies need to see that we do not believe Christ has abandoned us—or we him.

Others may yet again abuse our trust and take advantage of our care; it is almost certain that someone will. Yet those who are called to represent Jesus in an evil world extend the love that is in his heart even if doing so is certain to wound ours at some point. The apostle Peter explains, "For to this you have been called, because Christ also suffered for you, leaving you an example, so that you might follow in his steps" (1 Pet. 2:21).

We should be realistic enough about humanity's flaws to refuse to base our happiness on others' faithfulness. We should also be so focused on the cross as never to doubt our God's providential and perpetual care.

The Denial of Evil

We must refuse to believe that Jesus has abandoned us because some of his people have. We cannot believe the lie that our Savior has turned from us because our circumstances have turned sour. Whenever we are tempted to doubt God's care, we turn our eyes to Calvary and rest our souls on the undeniable truth proven there: "He cares for me!"

In the working-class church in which I began ministry, I learned from the hard lives of miners and farmers how Christ's cross prepared them for daily trial and regular tragedy. They told the story of a young man made an invalid by a mining accident caused by the employer's negligence. As his peers prospered, built homes, and raised families, the man grew old in the shack crumbling about him without such blessings.

One day a young man approached the old and asked, "Why do you believe that God loves you despite all of the evil that has hurt you?" The old man smiled and said, "Yes, it is true that sometimes

Satan comes to my bedside and points out my window to the men with whom I worked that now have families, homes, and health that I do not share. Then, Satan, says to me, 'Does Jesus really love you?'"

The honesty of the invalid took the young man by surprise. He asked with a gasp, "What do you say to Satan, when he asks you that question?"

Said the old man, "I take Satan by the hand and lead him to a hill called Calvary. There I point to the thorns on the brow, the nails in the hands and feet, and the spear-pierced side, and I say, 'Doesn't Jesus love me!'"

The Confession of Evil

We need Calvary's vital image of our God's abiding and eternal care not only because others betray Christ's purposes, but because we do. Much in this chapter has dealt with the wrong that others may do to us in our work. However, we must also face the truth of Scripture that says, "No temptation has overtaken you that is not common to man" (1 Cor. 10:13).

There was a time in my early Christian life that I took comfort from this verse, believing it meant that other people in the world shared whatever anger, despair, or lust was in me. That's true, and somewhat relieving. After all, misery loves company. I am happy not to be so weird as to be the only one sinning in these ways. I needed to learn, however, that there is far more comfort *and* conviction in these words from the apostle Paul.

If there is no sin that is not common to humanity, then it is true not only that my anger, despair, and lust are shared by others, but that I also share their sin. Our sin is *common*—universal.

I am not saying that all of us have actually murdered someone or committed adultery, but Jesus said that hatred is spiritual murder and lust is adultery of the heart (Matt. 5:21–30).

No sin of the flesh or spirit is unique to any person or completely absent from any person. Not all variations and degrees of sin have been expressed by every person, but the seed of every sin already exists in every heart. If this is difficult to accept, then we need to reconsider the words of James, the brother of Jesus: "Whoever keeps the whole law but fails in one point has become guilty of all of it" (James 2:10).

No one is experiencing a sin that is not also present in me in some rudimentary or raging form. Whether in seed form or full bloom, the essence of all sin already resides in my heart.

Because of our fallen nature, all of us who are ready to judge the wrongs of others will also be guilty of some dimension of the same (Matt. 7:2). No employee or supervisor works hard all the time. Our own computers wander to social media during work hours. Our coffee breaks run long. Whether we are captains of industry or sailors swabbing the decks after a supervisor's mess, we all find ways of taking advantage of others.

The most diligent among us waffle between workaholism and living for the weekends. We fudge on our expense accounts and make petty complaints. We love our spouses and lust for the attractive coworker or delivery driver. We find escape from work pressure by fantasizing about other careers, better bosses, or higher video-game scores.

Two important truths flow from this understanding of our common failings. First, I am in as much need of the cleansing blood of Jesus as those who have betrayed, abandoned, or hurt me. Friends were shocked when a well-known and highly respected Christian leader took them beneath the veneer of his public conduct to confess his continuing need of a Savior:

> I write these words at the age of fifty-five. During the past ten or twelve years, I have often—and with greater seriousness than ever before—reflected upon the course of my life. Certain patterns of thought and attitude and conduct have come to light, some of them quite disturbing. I look back upon repeated failures in my efforts to subdue inner thoughts, conflicts and fears, to combat immaturity and self-centeredness, to build genuine and enriching relationships with other people, to conquer besetting sins, and to grow in holiness and communion with God. I now see that every period of my life has been marked by . . . struggle. But the persistence of the failures, together with a growing understanding of the past, has made the struggles of recent years exceptionally intense and painful.[6]

Such sin is in my heart—and yours. It continues to hurt our Savior and grieve his Spirit even more than what we have experienced through the evil of others. We are in as much daily need of the grace of Jesus as they.

The second truth is this: those believers who have done evil to us are as much loved as we by our Savior. The commonness of our sin should make us less willing to judge, hate, and belittle others who need the same grace we do and receive it at the cost of Jesus's blood.

The degree of our sin may vary, but the necessity of Christ's grace for everyone's salvation does not. The greatness of our Savior's sacrificial love for us should make us willing to love those he loves, even if that requires fresh sacrifice from us. We lay our bitterness, hatred, resentment, pain, and desire for retribution upon the altar of his purposes because he laid down his life for us.

The essence of Christian obedience lies in Christ's words: "If you love me, you will keep my commandments" (John 14:15). Our love for him makes us want to obey his commands. So, what is his greatest command? He told us: "Love the Lord your God with all your heart and with all your soul and with all your mind" (Matt. 22:37).

Our obedience hinges on loving Christ above all other loves and with all that can express our love. So if we love Christ above all others, what will characterize our love? We will love those he loves. Whom does Jesus love? He loves the outcast, the oppressed, tax collectors, prostitutes, foreigners, thieves, murderers, our neighbors, our bosses, our betrayers, and, yes, our enemies. Love of him requires us to love them too (Matt. 5:44). That's why Jesus said that the second greatest commandment is like the first: "You shall love your neighbor as yourself" (Matt. 22:38).

My solidarity with other sinners is a consequence not just of our mutual sin but of our shared need of a Savior and of his love for those whose sin is "common." Such a perspective drains pride and bitterness from my heart and replaces the drumbeat of constantly rehearsed pain and desired retribution with the echoes of Christ's pardon. That echo increasingly drowns out the pounding hurt as I remember the greatness of his grace toward me that stirs such love for him and those he died to save.

I do not have to abandon a desire for justice or vindication to honor my Savior, but in their pursuit, I must seek his help to empty my heart of bitterness or rage that would damage his purposes.

It has often been said that unforgiveness is the acid that destroys its own container. So any pursuit of righteousness or restitution must be without resentment. Any form of hatred—even that arising from undeserved and unjust hurt—damages us, making our hearts hard and allowing those who once hurt us to further damage our relationships.

The Forgiveness of Evil

We should not fail to forgive because we have confused forgiveness and pardon. Biblical forgiveness does not require that we pardon (i.e., shelter from all consequences) those who have hurt us or others. Biblical forgiveness seeks what is best for the eternity of the wrongdoer and the flourishing of our community. Christ calls us to forgive out of a desire to extend God's blessings to the unsaved and undeserving. So even if justice and the security of others require that some not be pardoned of all consequences for their wrong, we still forgive them. Such forgiveness is not defined as ignoring or excusing evil but as having an attitude in our hearts that desires what is best for others' eternal good and for the expression of God's heart. To forgive is to be *for grace*.

Biblical forgiveness does not require removing all penalties for wrongdoing but the emptying of all malice in applying them. In our responses to personal hurt, we graciously consider whether it is best for the good of the wrongdoer and the common good that the consequences of wrongdoing be heavy or light or entirely removed (Mic. 6:8; 1 Pet. 4:8). Biblical forgiveness does not deny us the right to punish evil or work for its defeat, but the just consequences we seek should never be administered vindictively, without the ultimate good of the evildoer in mind.

The result of such a gospel response to evil is that it will not dominate us. When I am not brooding over how to get revenge or retribution for how I was wronged, my sleep is not disturbed with persistent dreams of what was said, what I wish I had said, or the final rhetorical sword stroke I hope to wield. My thoughts do not constantly dwell on how I will get even, and my heart is not freshly damaged by hating those who did evil to me in the past. In essence, biblical forgiveness seeks what is best even for those who have hurt us as we trust the Lord to vindicate our cause and exact the revenge that is his alone to repay (Ps. 138:8; Rom. 12:19).

As I conclude this chapter, it is important to note that I have mainly described the effects of evil on individuals in the workplace. I must not fail to indicate that evil knows no such boundaries. We are not prepared for the evil we will face and must oppose if we do not recognize that it can pervade a society through its work traditions, prejudices, memberships, and market policies.

We should not turn a blind eye to the awful burdens imposed on people of color or ethnic difference by real estate redlining, business loan practices, voting restrictions, educational inequities, imprisonment rates, and much more that has implications for individuals, families, opportunities, and occupations. Always there is the temptation to point to ancestors, politicians, and corporations as being responsible for such evil, but the sinful craving to be superior to someone resides in the dark places of every human heart.

God's people oppose evil not only by understanding how it invades individual souls but by recognizing how it can send its tentacles through the systems and customs of an entire society. Evil that is so pervasive and accepted can be hard to see and even harder to root out. The people best equipped to do so are those who recognize the evil our Savior must root out of us, and colabor with him in that work.

9

Leadership

AN INTERVIEWER GATHERED and questioned the eight former military aides to President Reagan. Each had taken a turn guarding the "football." The football is that attaché case that never leaves the presence of the president because it contains launch codes for our nation's nuclear weapons.

President Reagan's leadership was often distinguished by his communication skills but also by his humor. So the aides all smiled when the interviewer asked, "What did the president say when people asked him what was in that attaché case?"

They replied, "He always said the same thing. 'Inside there's a red button and a green button. The red button launches the nuclear weapons, and the green button averts the launch.' Then he would pause, look a bit quizzical, and ask, 'Or is it the other way around?'" That story reminds me that there are as many styles and flavors of leaders as there are responsibilities of leadership.

The Qualities of Leaders

While writing this chapter, I looked at all the books on my shelves about leadership, and I began to get weak in the knees. There's so much that could be said, so much that is expected, and so much that is required of leaders.

You could look at the qualifications the legendary business guru Peter Drucker said are important: good leaders work very hard and see their higher position as responsibility rather than privilege. Such leaders want strong, capable associates and motivate them by creating vision that inspires energy throughout a company, corporation, or institution.

Drucker emphasized the importance of leaders identifying a compelling vision for their organization. But it's also undeniable that visionary leaders have to rely on something other than reading the tea leaves of changing business environments to have lasting success. Business consultant Myron Rush adds that a true leader must be willing to stand alone and make decisions that others do not want to make.

Other writers add to the list of qualifications: leaders must strive for the best, always master their emotions, work hard, and maintain a balance of organizational energy, customer awareness, employee support, and self-care.

As I read that list of qualifications—and of course it could be longer—I doubt if anyone ever has the complete package. Given those high standards, who is really qualified to be a leader? I also wonder how that list of qualifications compares to the world's greatest leader, who rode into Jerusalem on a donkey's back to die for our sins.

I value the insights of the experienced leaders who catalog the characteristics and virtues of highly successful people. Yet the more I think about the qualities of leadership, the more I recognize that a biblical leader is someone who uses God's gifts to champion God's cause regardless of personal costs or challenging circumstances. Such leadership is far more about daily faithfulness than about a formula for success. The Christian commentator Cal Thomas writes about someone he knew who was that kind of leader:

> He had tremendous faith, but his wife was an alcoholic, and his daughter had psychological problems. The man himself was often in poor health. Yet week after week, he never complained. He always smiled and asked how I was doing when he saw me. He faithfully brought to church a young blind man and helped that man to sing the hymns by saying words into his ear. That man was a Christian leader if ever there was one.[1]

That Christian leader's example led Cal Thomas to write a noteworthy article entitled "Dear God, Please Don't Let Me Be a Christian Leader." After all, if being a leader requires pain and suffering and sacrifice for the sake of others, then we must be willing to pay a high price to lead as God intends. Paul writes about the kind of Christian leader who pays the price of daily faithfulness in 1 Thessalonians 5:12–15:

> We ask you, brothers, to respect those who labor among you and are over you in the Lord and admonish you, and to esteem them very highly in love because of their work. Be at peace

among yourselves. And we urge you, brothers, admonish the idle, encourage the fainthearted, help the weak, be patient with them all. See that no one repays anyone evil for evil, but always seek to do good to one another and to everyone.

Our Obligations toward Leaders

Curiously, the apostle does not start his discussion of organizational leadership with the qualifications of leaders. Rather, he talks about the obligations of people toward their leaders. What are the obligations that nourish the soil in which good leadership grows? The opening words, in 1 Thessalonians 5:12, answer that question: "We ask you, brothers, to respect those who labor among you." If we want to have good leaders over us, then our first obligation is to respect the leaders that God has put in place.

It shouldn't surprise us that there must be respect for leaders in order for organizations to flourish. Occasionally I have been able to ride in a military vehicle with my brother, who has been a military officer. I love the fact that when you're going through the gate of a military base with an officer, the guards salute you. I love being saluted! I recognize, of course, that the guards are not really saluting me. They're not even saluting my brother. They're saluting the insignia on the vehicle. The soldiers recognize that it's not the person, not even the qualities of the person, but rather the position that needs respect in order for the military to function well.

The same is true for those who hold political office. Even if we disagree with their policies, we recognize that our nation cannot function if there is not respect for its leaders. So the Bible tells us to pray for those in authority over us and to honor them (1 Tim. 2:1–3). There must be respect for leaders in order for organizations to fulfill their purposes.

In the verses cited above, Paul also tells the Thessalonians to esteem their church leaders "very highly in love because of their work." The translation "very highly" is actually three Greek verbs jammed into one, as if to say, "I want you to super-hyper esteem them!" The word Paul uses here (and in Ephesians 3:20) is coined for the first time in all known Greek literature. Paul creates it to emphasize just how much we should esteem our leaders for the church to function as it should.

What does it mean to respect and esteem leaders in the various contexts of life? Two Old Testament examples involving difficult leaders illustrate the biblical understanding.

The first example is found in the book of Daniel. The prophet Daniel served a proud and arrogant tyrant named Nebuchadnezzar, who ruled over God's people during their captivity in Babylon. Yet when Daniel interpreted the king's dreams about God's judgment against him, Daniel did so with the utmost respect, calling Nebuchadnezzar "My lord" and later citing his "greatness and glory and majesty" (Dan. 4:19; 5:18). Yet along with these signs of respect, Daniel urged the king to repent of sin to avoid awful consequences. The prophet speaks to the king out of a heart of personal respect that includes courageous compassion.

The second example is a young girl from Israel who was taken captive by Naaman, a Syrian general. When the girl found out that Naaman had leprosy, she said to Naaman's wife, "Would that my lord were with the prophet who is in Samaria! He would cure him of his leprosy" (2 Kings 5:3). Out of compassion and respect for the general who enslaved her, the servant girl began to minister in the name and for the purposes of God.

Sometimes it's difficult to show respect and esteem to those who lead us. But during such times, we need to remember that these are the qualities in which leaders can grow and thrive. Leaders are more likely to respect God's standards and fulfill his purposes when God's people reflect his character and respect his leaders.

Paul also nourishes the soil in which good leadership grows by telling his readers, "Be at peace among yourselves" (1 Thess. 5:13). Whether you're in a church, a corporation, or an educational institution, you know there are some people who are gifted at making people mad. They have the special ability to stir things up, and they seem to take delight in doing so. But when people start pulling apart rather than pulling together, leaders cannot do what they're supposed to do.

So Paul reminds us that good leadership benefits from a willingness of people in the organization to seek peace—to absorb insults, not to return evil for evil, and to work against the relational friction that keeps churches, companies, and institutions from functioning well. Leaders succeed because the people they lead seek peace.

Every sports comeback movie I can think of, whether *Hoosiers* or *Radio* or *Rudy*, begins with a new coach coming to lead a team of irritable misfits. At some point, there's a crisis where the coach wins the confidence in the team—and the team members put aside differences to follow their leader's directions. They can't reach their potential until they pull together and support the coach.

Do you remember when Jesus was ministering around Nazareth, and we are told that he could not do mighty works there? The reason given is that the people in his hometown did not believe in him or give him honor (Matt. 13:58). Obviously, Jesus still had divine power, but the passage reminds us that God chooses to work among people whose hearts are pulling in the same direction—his direction. When God's people are at peace with one another and their hearts are engaged in a common purpose, both the church and its leaders can thrive.

The organizational dynamics that establish good leadership in the church are not intended only for church. Christians are to be salt and light at work as well as followers of Christ at church. So supporting leaders by offering them respect and seeking peace with coworkers is part of our mission at work also. That just makes good sense. Since good leaders must unite institutions, companies, corporations, and churches in a common purpose, the people who contribute to that purpose build the leadership that helps all succeed. All of us have a role and a duty to invest in that kind of leadership.

Leadership Requirements

In his message to the Thessalonians, Paul also describes what is required of leaders themselves. He says, "We ask you, brothers, to respect those who *labor* among you" (1 Thess. 5:12). Paul expects leaders to be laboring. Here is the first qualification of a Christian leader: to work hard. The word *labor* means "to work almost to the point of exhaustion." Leaders are to expend themselves for the sake of others in both the church and the workplace.

To Labor

The next two words after "labor" in 1 Thessalonians 5:12 are "among you," and they identify another leadership characteristic.

Paul expects that Christian leaders will work and see themselves in the context of others' lives. Biblical leaders do not let their hard work isolate them from others or blind them to others' needs.

If you are a leader, it's not just about you.

It's not just about your promotion.

It's not just about your self-interest.

You are called to serve others. Biblical leadership exists for the benefit of others and requires understanding that God intends for leaders to be an instrument of his blessing in others' lives.

During the Protestant Reformation, the Reformers realized that God assigns certain gifts of leadership to the entire church. They expressed this with the phrase "the priesthood of believers." In the church of God's design, priests aren't the only ones with spiritual responsibilities—every believer is a priest, pointing others to God.

Part of that priesthood involves praying for and ministering to others in a church context, but we are also to take responsibility for others' needs and development in every sphere of our influence. We are not just priests among church people, but among all people that God calls his own and is seeking to reach with his grace. Whether you are a preacher, an executive in a corporate office, or a foreman on a road crew, your mission is to remember others' needs in order to advance Christ's purposes in their lives.

Martin Luther spoke about the church being "God's mouth house," the place in which the word of God is declared to his people. But the church also speaks outward to the world as her people demonstrate Christ's values in the workplace. To make the point that the preacher is only one of the people responsible for such proclamation, John Calvin sat among the people in his congregation on a common chair before he went up to a high pulpit to preach. He was making the point that the preacher is just like everyone else in having a responsibility to make Christ's blessings known. Christian leaders who recognize that they are called to be priests to their communities, companies, and crews labor "among" their people to help all flourish as God intends.

To Lead

Of course, the priesthood of believers does not remove the God-given authority of church leaders. The words in 1 Thessalonians 5:12 continue: "Respect those who labor among you *and are over you in the Lord.*" When Paul speaks of leaders being "over you," he uses a Greek word for authority that carries with it the notion of shepherding, guarding, and caring for those for whom one is responsible. This special term reminds us, again, that leaders are to use their authority for the good of others. Their supervision should never be self-oriented.

Paul reminds leaders in verse 12 that their supervision is also "in the Lord." That expression describes our union with Christ and is used nearly three hundred times in the epistles of Paul to describe how Jesus's identity becomes our own. When we supervise people "in the Lord," we represent him—his priorities, his character, and his righteousness.

Of course, that would be really tough if it were all dependent on our grit and resolve. To act with priestly concern for those whose values and actions may be contrary to God may require a tough love that no one else understands. Our union with Christ, in which his word and Spirit enable us to make tough decisions that represent him in a world often opposed to him, prepares us for the priestly pain that true leadership may require.

William Willimon is a Christian writer and church executive who wrote to explain why so many leaders without this priestly perspective cannot endure the pain biblical leadership requires. He relates the following:

> In high school, I worked at a failing sporting goods store. This youthful brush with business convinced me I was unsuited for commercial life. I realized bosses must hire and fire people, cut costs, reprimand unproductive employees and have uncomfortable conversations. I was too nice to do that. . . . [But] twenty years later, knee deep in a congregational crisis [I realized] leadership is only necessary . . . if an organization needs to go somewhere and is accountable for some mission more important that its survival. . . . A real leader . . . induces pain—the pain the organization has been studiously avoiding.[2]

Honestly, that doesn't sound very Christlike. To manage, no, more than manage, to *lead* organizations, we must recognize that we are being called to bring pain into people's lives.

Any organization can continue to run (or run down) as it presently is. The calling of leaders is to stretch an organization beyond its present limitations, limitations that are caused by practices, policies, and priorities that will ultimately choke the organization if not corrected.

Yet such stretching must occur at the same time those limitations are being studiously protected by those in the organization who for various reasons—that are not necessarily evil—do not want the changes to occur. This means that the good of the organization requires that the leader risk rejection, even sacrifice, for the sake of others. That's what makes true leadership Christlike and requires Christian leaders to know and depend upon their Lord to weigh the degree, timing, and intensity of change that accomplishes Christ's ends with Christ's priorities and people in mind.

God calls for leaders who will lead his people "in the Lord" (5:12). That means biblically oriented leaders should be united to Christ's purposes and character. Their actions should be righteous. They should be caring and selfless. Their efforts should be bathed in prayer, knowing that without Christ's standards and support, their leadership will either crush them or crush those they lead.

To Admonish

The end of verse 12 tells God's people that their leaders are not only "over you in the Lord," but are also called to, uh-oh, "admonish you." The word translated as "admonish" is from the Greek word *noutheteo*, which means "to set the mind." When facing opposition to our ideas, we may sometimes speak about needing to make our point by "setting people's thinking straight" or changing their minds. That's the essential idea behind this Greek word. Some Christians may already be familiar with this word because it's behind an approach to Christian counseling known as "nouthetic counseling," which seeks to use biblical principles to change people's thoughts and habits.

In this passage, Paul is saying that leaders must sometimes be willing to admonish those under their care to set their minds and habits on a different course. This does not mean that leaders don't care about others. Rather, because Christian leaders care about those under their authority, they work hard to reset and reorient minds and hearts toward goals consistent with an organization's good and God's values.

Leaders know their people cannot do what God intends for their lives or the organization they serve without right application of their talents and energies. So responsible leaders admonish irresponsibility, dishonesty, laziness, and bad attitudes. That means that there may need to be correction for wrong practices or consequences for performance that does not measure up to what is good and necessary for the organization to take care of its business and others' needs.

In the same passage that we have been considering, Paul says, "We urge you, brothers, admonish the idle" (5:14). Nobody wants to do that, but in the very next letter to the Thessalonians, Paul writes even more strongly: "If anyone is not willing to work, let him not eat" (2 Thess. 3:10). Whoa, there's a consequence! If you're not going to work, you don't get to eat. That's admonishment!

No one should like taking such measures, but godly leaders do not avoid such responsibilities when needed for the good of others. Neither the individual nor the organization on whose health they and others subsist gains from leadership that ignores wrong, irresponsible, or incompetent work.

When I was working at an educational institution, I was chosen by my peers, who were other faculty members, to become the new dean of faculty. In other words, I was to become their boss. As some readers may know, one of the hardest places to be a boss is where you supervise those who were once your peers (and some had even been my professors). They may still love you, but they may not love it when you have to make them face the consequences of their actions.

I remember a man I loved and worked with who would not do what was required of him despite admonishments, instructions, and even reprimands. I had many sleepless nights wrestling with how to handle his actions and antics. During the night, I had all kinds of debates with myself. *What do I do with this person? How can I resolve this situation?* I was really struggling. After all, he was a believer. I loved him. I wanted to be compassionate and caring toward him. But he was not doing his job, and he was not willing to change!

Finally, the president of the organization came to me and said, "Bryan, aren't you a man of faith? Don't you believe that God can put that man in a position that is appropriate for his gifts? It is not loving to keep someone in a position to which God has not called him."

At that point I realized that the person I was most trying to protect was *me*. Yes, I also wanted to protect the employee and the peace of the organization, but most of all I wanted to spare myself pain.

I didn't want the pain of admonishing wrong.

I didn't want the difficulty of correcting.

I didn't want to deal with the terrible awkwardness of having to discipline, or even fire, a friend.

The reality was that the man had demonstrated that he could not do the job the school required. So, I had to face the truth that it isn't loving to keep somebody in a job for which God has not called that person. I needed to act with the faith that God had gifted that man for a different calling that was according to God's purposes (Eph. 2:10). Further, I needed to believe God would still love me, even if others stopped liking me. My leadership required confidence in God's continued care more than in others' continuing approval.

To Encourage

Though it may require tough decisions, biblical leadership is not all about admonishing others. Paul tells leaders not only to admonish the idle but to "encourage the fainthearted" (1 Thess. 5:14).

The Greek word for "fainthearted" is formed from two words that mean "small" and "soul." So in one sense, Paul is telling us to encourage those whose souls are small. Sometimes the pressures of life can figuratively shrink people's souls. Discouragement dries up their faith or shrivels their joy. A job or a family issue may have hurt them in such a way that they need to be built up again or reinvigorated. They may need hope that things can be different. For all these reasons and many more, leaders are called to encourage the fainthearted.

Paul also tells leaders to "help the weak" (5:14). Sometimes people need more training. Some need more resources. Some need a coach. Some need others to support them. If you're a biblical leader, you are also obligated to try to understand how you can help people receive the encouragement and the help they may need to fulfill God's calling on their lives.

To Be Patient

Finally, Paul instructs leaders, "Be patient with them all" (5:14). We must give people time to change and to grow. Our patience with those we supervise should demonstrate the character of the God we serve. He is patient with us—slow to anger and abounding in steadfast love (Ex. 34:6).

How patience works itself out in the workplace is usually demonstrated by consistent fairness. We reflect the grace we ourselves need when we are patient in our leadership. When correction is needed, Christian leaders objectively evaluate performance, give people the opportunity to change, and then reevaluate (including evaluating whether to begin this cycle again)—a process that requires patience.

We should not admonish without first clarifying expectations, explaining a process of evaluation, warning of potential consequences, encouraging whenever possible, and patiently offering help for success, as much as possible. Why expend so much energy? God wants us to give people the opportunity to grow and change. We are priests in the workplace for the people that are precious to God. He wants us to treat others the way we desire to be treated and the way we need our Lord to treat us (Matt. 7:12).

Helping People to Flourish

If we summarize all the leadership principles that the apostle has talked about—lead by example, admonish the idle, encourage the fainthearted, help the weak, be patient with them all—we recognize that they are designed to help people flourish in the calling God gives them.

In *When Helping Hurts*, Brian Fikkert writes, "The goal of human flourishing is to restore people to full expression of humanness, to bring what God created us to be in right relationship with him."[3] I doubt that many business schools would think of leadership this way, but as believers our responsibility is to help people come into right relationship with God so that they can flourish both now and eternally. If you're a champion of the cause of Christ, then that is part of your mission.

You may be thinking, "But I've got an awful boss who doesn't encourage the fainthearted, or help the weak, and he isn't patient with his employees." That may be the case, and that's why Paul includes this instruction: "See that no one repays anyone evil for evil" (1 Thess. 5:15). That's so hard if you've been hurt or belittled or even damaged by other people. Our reflexive response is to get even by treating others the way they treat us. But what does that accomplish?

If unforgiveness begins to pervade your heart, then you've given somebody else leadership over your soul. Their sin is now ruling your thoughts, dreams, and attitudes. Their evil begins directing your heart. But when we forgive those who have hurt us, we are saying to ourselves and to God's people, "I will not be controlled by evil." Yes, abusive behavior and unjust treatment should be confronted and corrected, but even then, the rule of righteousness rather than revenge must be our goal.

Two Christian businesspeople I know co-own a small business. They have discovered that part of the business plan of some larger businesses is to bring suits against smaller companies. These aggressor businesses recognize that if they can drain enough time, energy, and money from the smaller companies, then ultimately their lawsuits will break the smaller companies and open up markets for the larger businesses' products.

The initial tendency of the Christian business owners was to hate the other businesses and to create an atmosphere of hate toward them within their company. Then they began to recognize that their employees were blaming the losses of the company on the larger businesses rather than on their own performance or productivity. More importantly, the business owners realized that as Christians they needed to teach and demonstrate Christ's forgiveness—not just to keep people working hard but to reflect the character of Christ.

That takes us to the final standard that Paul holds up for Christians and Christian leaders: "Always seek to do good to one another and to everyone" (5:15). I'm so glad that Paul uses the word *seek*. This is the *goal* we aspire to achieve. We do our best to be salt and light in our culture, our company, or our institution to bring God's priorities into the world.

We may strike out a lot. We may not be accomplishing all that God wants us to do. But we continue to pursue his goals. That's what our hearts long for. We *seek* the good of others so that they can flourish in the way that God intends and discover his heart for humanity.

One of the most influential books of recent decades for Christian leaders is James Davison Hunter's little work with a big title: *To Change the World*. Hunter asks Christian leaders, "What is God calling you to do?" Yes, you can read all the leadership qualifications in the multitude of business books, and they may provide good, helpful advice for daily habits and duties. But Hunter says that God ultimately calls each of us to be "a faithful presence" in the place of our profession.[4]

The great Christian scholar and statesman Abraham Kuyper famously said, "There is not a square inch in the whole domain of our human existence over which Christ, who is Sovereign over *all*, does not cry: 'Mine!'" As believers, we are called to say, "In whatever square inch God has assigned me, I'm called to be a faithful presence in that place. That means that I am not only called to have faith in Christ but also to reflect his humility, his courage, his forgiveness, his patience, and his desire that all should flourish according to his will for them."

When that is our goal, we can change the world one square inch at a time.

10

Balance

AN ELEMENTARY SCHOOL teacher told her class, "Draw a picture of something your father does every day." One child drew stick figures of a family seated around a breakfast table, except for the father, who was running out the door. There were balloon captions over the heads of all the children seated at the kitchen table, and each had the same words: "Hurry, Daddy, hurry!"

The child who drew the picture was my son, and the father heading out the door in such a hurry was me. My son's drawing revealed his perception and at the same time cut me to the heart. I had to ask myself the question, Why is my son's most vivid image of me a portrayal of his father rushing away from him and the rest of his family every day?

I can offer all kinds of good explanations for why that was the case. I could say I was doing important work as a busy church executive. I was hustling to provide for my family. I was also fulfilling the important calling of training people for ministry. Yet I knew in my heart that if my son's primary image of his father was me running away from him, something was out of balance in my life.

As you read my story above, you may have realized that you face your own struggles to maintain a balanced life. In fact, this entire book may have increased those struggles. After all, I have emphasized that our work is a holy calling where we honor Christ in everything we do, whether it's a business meeting, an important project, or even a phone conversation. We bear the name of Christ and have obligations to reflect his character in the workplace. That can make us feel even more pressure! A friend of mine who felt the weight of his Christian calling once told me, "Whenever I sit down, I feel guilty."

Clearly that is not what God intends. That's why in this chapter I want to look at Psalm 127, which is about finding life's balance by focusing on God's priorities:

> Unless the LORD builds the house,
>   those who build it labor in vain.
> Unless the LORD watches over the city,
>   the watchman stays awake in vain.
>
> It is in vain that you rise up early
>   and go late to rest,
> eating the bread of anxious toil;
>   for he gives to his beloved sleep.
>
> Behold, children are a heritage from the LORD,
>   the fruit of the womb a reward.
> Like arrows in the hand of a warrior

are the children of one's youth.
Blessed is the man
　　who fills his quiver with them!
He shall not be put to shame
　　when he speaks with his enemies in the gate.

A Pointless Theme

The theme of this psalm is announced in verse 1: "Unless the LORD builds the house, those who build it labor in vain." What is the core truth in that theme? Without God's blessing, our work is pointless.

You may think that you can simply hone your talents and increase your energy so that your life will prosper. But just a little hiccup in the economy, just a mistaken entry in a ledger, just a brief change of circumstances—a car crosses a center line for a fraction of a second, you breathe in a microscopic virus, your child takes a wrong step—and life as you know it comes unraveled more quickly and deeply than you ever believed was possible.

The Lord deals with these realities in this psalm that, in essence, tells us, "You can dedicate yourself to the work that needs to be done or to the God who gets the job done." His priorities are made clear even in the opening words, where he is referred to as "the LORD." In most Bibles, the word "LORD" in this psalm has every letter capitalized to indicate it is a translation of the Hebrew name Jehovah.

Jehovah is the Lord Almighty.

Jehovah is the Creator of the heavens and the earth.

The heavens are Jehovah's throne; the earth is his footstool.

By Jehovah's hand all things hold together.

Jesus is the manifestation of Jehovah's glory, and one day every knee will bow and every tongue confess that he is Lord (Phil. 2:10–11).

Jesus Is Lord of All

If Jesus really is Lord over all things, then Abraham Kuyper's statement that every square inch of creation belongs to Christ takes on added significance. We are not only expected to crown Jesus as Lord of all someday in a heavenly future; we are required to acknowledge his dominion over all things every day.

That means we can never exclude him from any space or time in our lives. We do not say to him, "Jesus, you can be Lord of my life in church, but the workplace is mine, and I'm the one who makes things happen there." No, he is Lord over all, or he is not Lord at all.

There is a genuine busyness that flows from dedicated devotion to God's purposes. But it's not a devotion that excludes him. Biblical balance keeps us available to God. Hellish busyness makes us unavailable to God. We are off course when we think to ourselves: *I'm too busy for the niceties of honoring God. I can't be bothered with prayer. There is no space in my schedule for devotions or worship. I don't have the luxury of time to consider what God's word says about this decision.*

No, if it's biblically balanced busyness, then I should always have time for a spoken prayer to God, or at least a thought arrow requesting his help before I pick up the phone for an important conversation, or type a memo for a meeting, or plan a conversation with a coworker.

If my business decisions allow no time for counsel from God's word or a Christian friend, then I am being ruled by a schedule that has put God on the sidelines of my life. What's the problem with that? Read the opening words of Psalm 127 again: "Unless the LORD builds the house . . ." Biblical busyness does not exclude biblical habits or spiritual disciplines.

All of us need the opportunity to ask ourselves, *Is what I'm about to do truly going to honor God? Will this demonstrate God's priorities to the people I work for or who work for me? Are my actions an appropriate expression of God's character and care? Am I available to God in the way my work is being done? Is what I am doing or planning to do consistent with the principles of Scripture?*

We can get so preoccupied with our work that we fail to make ourselves available to the God who makes it possible and fruitful. So the psalmist challenges us here, saying that unless God builds the house we're working in vain, even if we bring all our talents and efforts to the table.

A Song for the Journey

What makes us involve God in our work other than feeling guilty if we don't? Part of the answer is found in the heading or superscription of Psalm 127, which reminds us of its source and purpose. The heading reads, "A Song of Ascents."

This psalm was written by Solomon for a very specific purpose. As pilgrims came into Jerusalem and began to ascend Mount Zion, going up to the temple to worship and praise God, this is one of the songs they would sing. Though the people were singing about their work, they were pulling away from their daily labors for a time of worship.

This context of the psalm reminds us that because the Lord had constantly made himself available to these people, they were setting aside time for his worship. They prioritized approaching him because he had been present for them. Despite their sins and failings, he had sustained them through troubles and trials. His constant presence was both the cause of their praise and the assurance that they could rest from their labors to honor him.

God is also present for us in our place of work. That's why we can approach him there at all times in prayer and rest from our labors long enough to honor him. He can take care of things while we worship. Dedicating ourselves to God is not a disadvantage. The time spent in praise is not wasted. Since the Lord is responsible for our livelihood and our family's welfare, we have no more important task than uniting our hearts to him. Being reminded that we are his beloved and that he controls all things for our eternal benefit is good for our blood pressure as well as for a business that needs employees and employers not controlled by anxiety.

The assurance we need to find balance in our lives is the gospel, which this psalm makes apparent in a nutshell: a loving Lord has made a way for us to come to him. When that truth begins to hit you, a certain awe comes into your heart: *He shouldn't care about me. He's got a universe to run. Yet the Lord loves me and has made a way for me to come to him; more than that, he invites me to involve him in every aspect of my life so that I can rest in the confidence that the tough problems and people are in his control.*

When you begin to treasure what God has done for you, then you want to involve him—for reasons more than guilt—in your workplace. He has your best interests in mind. He loves you enough to send his Son for you. He promises that he will work for eternal good whatever earthly work you do. He promises in his word, "I've got this." So you can rest from the drivenness that comes from thinking you've got to have a handle on everything, every moment. And the very reason that you can be so energized for the hard work he calls you to do is that you're so well rested in his care.

Awesome Sleep

Kathy and I have friends who are missionaries in the Muslim portions of the Philippines. At times their work is not only difficult but dangerous. Not long ago, I received a very moving letter from one of the missionaries, whose name is Rene Quimbo. Here's what he wrote:

> We heard gunshots the other day and the sounds of running feet as people rushed by our ministry center. The coffee and the rubber farms were on fire. We were in shock, because we were told it was most likely intentionally done. We were upset, but we lifted everything to God who holds everything together. Many tears were shed, but we prayed that what people intended for evil God would work for good. We don't know how, but because God is good, it should work out so. So, we could sleep.

The last words of his letter echo Psalm 127:2: "He gives to his beloved sleep." I love to hear people say, "I was struggling with anxiety, and then I decided to turn it over to God." When you really do turn your concerns over to the one who creates and controls all things—with trust in his love for you—there is a wonderful result in your life: you can sleep.

The psalmist is telling us that awe is the antidote to anxiety. If we're awed by the fact that Almighty God loves us and that he's working all things toward our best interests, then we really can be free from anxiety. Isaiah 26:3 tells us, "You keep him in perfect peace whose mind is stayed on you, because he trusts in you." Isn't that wonderful? If our minds are focused on the Lord Jehovah, then our hearts can be at peace.

Two Types of People

Of course, there are other ways that people can approach the problems that make us anxious. Psalm 127:2 describes the approaches of two different types of people. One is addicted to activity. These are the workaholics, and they are addressed in the first half of the verse: "It is in vain that you rise up early and go late to rest." These people are the early birds, getting a jump on things. And they are the night owls, who work until late in the evening. In other words, they are workaholics, burning the candle at both ends.

Of course, there have been workaholics throughout history. I smile, remembering the story of an ancient Greek named Demosthenes. He was a statesman who worked against corruption in Greece. He worked night and day, thinking that if he ever stopped, the world would fall apart. To ensure that he would keep at his job, he shaved half of his head so he would be too embarrassed to go out in public.

But workaholism is not the only sign of a life out of balance. Some people are anxiety addicts. They feed off anxiety because it gives them the energy they need to engage the tasks before them.

Several years ago, my family went to a Christian conference that provided us housing in a condo on the seashore. When we walked in the front door, we faced a picture window that framed the beautiful seascape. The view was incredible. But when one of our daughters saw the ocean, she said, "Oh, no! Now a hurricane can get us." We replied, "There is no hurricane. Enjoy the ocean." But guess what? By the end of the week, there was a hurricane!

Sometimes anxiety pays off, right? If I'm anxious, my worry may motivate me to plan very carefully or work at a frantic pace, and these approaches to work can be beneficial for a time. But some people never can stop worrying because their anxiety is the fuel of their drivenness, even as it empties their souls of happiness.

There is nothing wrong with hard work, serious assessment of problems, and careful planning for solutions. But the faithlessness that drives workaholism and addictive anxiety is what the Scriptures warn against.

Freedom from Fear

Often the difference between responsible planning and destructive anxiety is what's driving our activity. So that we will know the difference, it's important to discern our own personality drivers. Often for the workaholic or the anxiety addict, a fear of the loss of stuff is the primary concern: "I have to build this house or I won't have nice things. I have to build this business or lose my livelihood. I have to build my reputation or lose others' respect." The pressure to avoid loss drives our motivation to build, and our burdens mount because everything we hold dear seems to depend upon the performance that secures our stuff or status.

The antidote to that kind of workaholism and anxiety is to trust that our God is in control of the universe and our corner of it. He owns the cattle on a thousand hills and treasures us.

He guides the nations and provides for our family. He loves our children more than we do. He loves me more than I can fathom. And because he is my Lord, he will provide what I need the most for my eternal good.

When fear of the loss of status fuels our drivenness, we are actually doubting our significance: "If I don't keep going, I won't get the promotion I need to be important. If I don't get that position or recognition, then my parents will be ashamed of me. My spouse will not respect me. I won't have the regard of my peers." We become driven by the need to maintain our significance before others rather than resting in the assurance of our treasured status secured by our Savior.

Comedian Jim Carrey, who starred in the movies *Liar Liar* and *Bruce Almighty*, made some amazingly insightful statements about personal significance at one of the Golden Globe Awards programs. Here's what he said about himself before he presented the award:

> I am two-time Golden Globe winner Jim Carrey. You know, when I go to sleep at night, I'm not just a guy going to sleep. I'm two-time Golden Globe winner Jim Carrey going to get some well-needed shuteye. And when I dream, I don't just dream any old dream. No, sir. I dream about being three-time Golden Globe–winning actor Jim Carrey. Because then I would be enough. It would finally be true, and I could stop this terrible search for what I know ultimately won't fulfill me.[1]

In a moment of candor, Carrey spoke the truth: if we keep on trying to find significance in what other people think or what we can accumulate, we ultimately discover our accolades and achievements will never be enough to keep us satisfied.

Pastor and writer Tim Keller encourages us to consider what is "the work under the work" that we do.[2] Don't just think about the work that you do. What is working on you that's driving you? Fear of loss of significance? Fear of losing reputation, luxury, relationships, or respect?

Whatever it is, such fears spell a loss of the gospel, because they are triggered by forgetting the God who constantly says to us, "I don't love you because of what you have accomplished; I love you because I've given my Son for you, and you've put your faith in him. Because your faith is in him, you have his identity before me. You are my precious child. I will take care of you as I know is best for earth and for eternity. Because you are mine, not only do I love you; I give you the significance of a purpose and calling in life so that you can respond in gratitude and thanksgiving to the wonder of my heart's claim upon you."

The gospel should free us from the fear of insignificance due to the loss of stuff or status. We can take some time off and balance our priorities because God loves us. Whatever we're worried about, he will provide as he knows is absolutely best for our eternity.

So instead of fueling my work with anxiety, I have the privilege of saying to myself, *God's got this. It's in his hands.* So get some rest and wake up refreshed and ready to tackle life's challenges with the courage and energy that come from confidence in him.

Learning to Rest

One of the evidences of imbalance in our lives is that we can't rest. There are many things in society that can keep us from rest.

One of the main culprits is technology. It is supposed to make our lives easier, and in some ways it does. But let me make an honest confession. I can remember when I loved getting on a plane, and the reason was that there were no phones, no texts, no emails. My airplane seat was the one place in my vocational existence that I could get some mental and emotional space. Now what have the airline geniuses done to me? They put Wi-Fi on the planes! So I can no longer escape. Rest is even harder to find.

Researchers at Oxford University say that technology causes us to be available twenty-four hours a day—not just to our boss but to our social media friends. So what's the last thing we do before we go to bed at night? Check our messages. And if we wake up in the middle of the night, what do we do? Check Facebook, Instagram, or the current equivalent. We are so addicted to our phones that we can't turn them off even at night. I read an article recently that was entitled, "What Would Jesus Do with a Smartphone?" Of course, I don't know for sure. But I think he would turn it off occasionally!

More and more we are discovering the real wisdom of the biblical notion of a Sabbath rest, that God can do more good with our lives in six days than we can do in seven days of nonstop labor. The Sabbath is, among other things, a declaration of freedom and a sign of a balanced life.

Even businesses know that if you don't rest, you can't work, which is why many require their employees to take their vacation days. Employers even track schedules to see whether workers have taken their vacation days, because the companies know that if we don't take time off, we will become unproductive. This business practice actually reflects a biblical principle that God encouraged us to embrace long ago: if we do not rest, we cannot work. Taking a Sabbath is not only good for life's balance; it's good for vocational excellence.

What gives us the ability to rest? Remembering that the Lord who made the universe and loved us enough to send his Son for us has our best interests at heart and our situation under control. Whatever is troubling us or challenging us is not beyond God's control. He has made himself available to you, he is watching over you, and because he's got this (whatever it is), you can rest in the assurance of his power and provision.

Seasons of Life

Our ability to rest despite our personalities or pressures also depends on understanding that there are various seasons in life that God will take us through. There are intense seasons such as when we're in grad school or our family is expanding or our business is in a growth spurt, and then it's true—we can't let up for a time. But that's not the long-term pattern of life that God intends for us. Different priorities must rule in different seasons.

Some time ago, my wife, Kathy, was on a panel of minister's wives. A question came from one of the people in the audience: What are the obligations of the pastor's wife?

One of the first women on the panel to speak was the wife of a senior statesmen in our denomination. She replied, "If you're a pastor's wife, you need to be at church every time the doors are open. In fact, you need to be there before the doors open and stay until they are closed. Your responsibility is to support your spouse in every ministry activity."

As she was talking, the other wives on the panel began to look at one another with concern. Finally, they said, "We've got to talk about what you just said." As they talked, everyone began to recognize that the wife who first spoke was an empty nester. She had no nursing babies, no carpools to drive, and no soccer games to attend. She and her husband were able to devote themselves entirely to church work because of their season of life. The others on the panel were in a very different season of life with very different demands.

Different seasons of life are very appropriate reasons for us to reevaluate our pressures and rethink priorities. One of those seasons is mentioned in Psalm 127: "Behold, children are a heritage from the LORD, the fruit of the womb a reward. Like arrows in the hand of a warrior are the children of one's youth. Blessed is the man who fills his quiver with them!" (vv. 3–5). The psalmist recognizes that there is a season for raising children.

A Heritage from the Lord

The psalmist tells us that children are "a heritage from the LORD." The word *heritage* is the same word behind the concept of an inheritance. Usually you get an inheritance when somebody dies, but, of course, God isn't dying. Instead, he's reminding us that the children we receive are from him and remain his. We are stewards for a time of the precious and eternal souls God has put into our families. He has entrusted us with the responsibility of caring for this inheritance.

If we are to do this effectively, we need to assess our priorities and maintain a proper balance in our lives. We need to affirm that our family is more important than our business advancement. Our family is more important than our bank account. Our children are more important than our personal comfort or promotion. Why? Because our bank account and business status are not eternal; our children's souls are.

The psalmist says, "Like arrows in the hand of a warrior are the children of one's youth. Blessed is the man who fills his quiver with them!" (127:4). To be honest, I don't know how many "arrows" should be in a quiver. I think there's a reason the Bible does not give us a specific number. If it did, we would use that number to pressure couples to have a certain number of children or to make them feel guilty if they don't have enough kids.

The Bible is not doing that. There are different quiver capacities based upon age, health, and income, and these can affect our priorities. Not everybody is in the stage or position of life to have lots of children. We should never take Christian prudence out of the equation of family planning. The point of Scripture is that our children are ours only by provision of God's blessing, and treasuring those blessings enables us to discover many of life's most profound joys and spiritual priorities.

According to the psalmist, children are not merely precious; they are protection—not from earthly enemies but from Satan, who wants our lives to be out of balance as we fight for Christ's glory. In order to protect us, God puts precious "arrows" in our spiritual quivers to keep our priorities in balance. God intends for our love for our children rightly to motivate us to be responsible in raising those whom he has entrusted to us.

The spiritual priorities we pursue to nurture our children in Christ's love actually help protect us from the spiritual dangers of selfish, irresponsible, or work-addicted lives.

Freedom from Guilt

The spiritual benefits of a godly home are meant to encourage faithfulness and balance for all of our lives. But, to be honest, I often feel guilty whenever someone talks about the responsibilities parents have for their children. I know that I am not always in balance and can't get seem to get it all right for very long. No one can. That's why it's important that we remember that Psalm 127 is about God's provisions for his beloved. How could he love people who mess up so often? The answer to which all Scripture points is that God has provided forgiveness to us through Jesus Christ.

My son's drawing that I described at the beginning of this chapter is not the only one that I have kept. About ten years after my son drew his picture of me dashing out the door, our youngest daughter got the same assignment from her teacher—but the school had changed the question.

The original teacher had asked my son to draw an answer to, "What does my father do every day?" However, the question my daughter was asked is, "What do I like best about my daddy?"

I like that question better—it's safer. Also, when my daughter drew her pictures, she did not write, "Hurry, Daddy, hurry!" One of her captions said, "He plays games with me." A second was, "He makes good oatmeal." And her third caption was, "He jogs with me before supper." (That was before both my knee operations.)

There's a reason why I keep these pictures next to where I exercise in the mornings. I want to celebrate that by the grace of God, I have made some progress in a balanced life. There were faults that I needed to change. But God's grace was sufficient to give me new priorities and help me make progress in the way I relate to my children.

I've also discovered that God's grace in our hearts can become a fountain that overflows to our children, our grandchildren, our neighbors, and our coworkers. When they see the peace and joy and balance that faith in God's love brings to our lives, they are drawn to the blessings of a relationship with our Savior. The blessings of balance are ours by the grace of God, and they are ours to share so that others too might celebrate the goodness that gives his beloved rest.

11

Witness

A CHRISTIAN WOMAN in my congregation was working as a teller at a local bank during the Christmas season. She decided to give her coworkers a small Christian devotional book as a gift. As far as she could tell, absolutely nothing happened in their lives as a result. The heavens didn't open, and nobody fell to their knees in repentance.

But about five or six years later, a young woman approached her and said, "Do you remember me?" And the woman in our congregation, who no longer worked at the bank, spoke honestly, "No, I don't remember you." The young woman told her, "I was a substitute teller on the day that you gave out those devotionals to your fellow workers. And after reading the devotional, I received the Lord Jesus Christ as my Savior."

There are two remarkable things about that encounter. First, it reminds us that the Lord continues working behind the scenes even when we cannot see what he is doing. Second, because she's honest, the Christian woman who gave out the devotional said to me later, "What surprised me even more than this woman being moved by the devotional was that God used me in her life. I was not walking very closely with the Lord in those days." This story is a reminder that we don't have to be a perfect witness to be powerfully used by God.

Throughout this book, I have emphasized that every place we work is holy ground and that we have a vocation, a calling, to represent our Savior in the workplace. Our vocation is where we exercise our profession—both in terms of our training and our testimony.

But if we do share our faith publicly, what does the Bible say we can expect from others and from God? The words of Jesus from the Sermon on the Mount help us to answer that question. In Matthew 5:10–16, Jesus says the following:

Blessed are those who are persecuted for righteousness' sake, for theirs is the kingdom of heaven.

Blessed are you when others revile you and persecute you and utter all kinds of evil against you falsely on my account. Rejoice and be glad, for your reward is great in heaven, for so they persecuted the prophets who were before you.

You are the salt of the earth, but if salt has lost its taste, how shall its saltiness be restored? It is no longer good for anything except to be thrown out and trampled under people's feet.

You are the light of the world. A city set on a hill cannot be hidden. Nor do people light a lamp and put it under a basket, but on a stand, and it gives light to all in the house. In the same way, let your light shine before others, so that they may see your good works and give glory to your Father who is in heaven.

God's Promises Outweigh Our Problems

The first thing this passage tells us is that God's promises outweigh our problems. If we witness at work (or any other place), there will be problems. Jesus tells us clearly at the beginning of his sermon, "Blessed are those who are persecuted for righteousness' sake." He wants us to know that even when we're doing the right things, there can be hard or even cruel consequences.

Why would that be? Because if we are running crosscurrent to what the world expects or is doing, there can be a lot of turbulence. For example, every year the American Library Association compiles a list of the ten most challenged books in public libraries. This list is the result of documented requests to remove materials from schools or libraries. The list recently included not only *Fifty Shades of Grey* and *Two Boys Kissing* but also *The Holy Bible*. Why was the Bible included in the list? It was included because of its "religious viewpoint," which is increasingly unpopular in our culture.[1]

In the workplace, there are many ways that Christians can stand against the cultural currents that oppose Christ's standards. For example, what if all your coworkers are padding their expense reports for extra income, but you decide not to follow that practice? There may be some turbulence, because other people can start to look bad because of your ethical stance.

What happens if everyone at a medical clinic is approving procedures that are unnecessary or inaccurately coded to get greater insurance reimbursements? If you refuse to follow those practices, you create turbulence.

What if peers or bosses at your plant are all covering up quality-control issues? If you decide to take a stand against such deception, that can create turbulence. You may not just be in trouble; you might be considered a threat—and that could cost you your job.

These are not merely hypothetical examples. After a sermon I gave on this passage, a man in my church came to me and said, "If I don't do some of those things, people will say I'm not being a team player. If I don't go along with what others are doing, I will likely be fired simply for doing what is right."

If you're facing similar difficulties in the workplace, notice what Jesus says: "Blessed are you when others revile you and persecute you and utter all kinds of evil against you falsely on my account" (5:11). Jesus knows we will be persecuted for his sake, but he assures us that our problems are not greater than God's promises.

Jesus's Three Promises

Three promises are made in this passage to those who honor Christ in their witness and work: blessings, the kingdom, and good company.

The word *blessed* is used twice in verses 10 and 11. What are those blessings? One of them is reflected in the blessing originally mentioned in Numbers 6:24–26:

> The LORD bless you and keep you;
> the LORD make his face to shine upon you and be gracious
>   to you;
> the LORD lift up his countenance upon you and give you peace.

When Jesus promises to preserve his kingdom and provide reward for those who are persecuted for his sake, he maintains

God's commitment to bless and keep us in the ways best for our eternity.

There is only one occasion in human history when God forsook one of his children. That was when the Lord Jesus took our sin upon himself on the cross. The sky went dark, and Jesus cried out, "My God, my God, why have you forsaken me?" (Matt. 27:46). The Father's face of blessing went dark for his Son while he was on the cross so that his face could shine upon us forever. He does not turn away from us even when others do.

The second blessing that Jesus promises is the kingdom: "Blessed are those who are persecuted for righteousness' sake, for theirs is the kingdom of heaven." Notice the present tense: "Theirs *is* the kingdom of heaven" (Matt. 5:10). This isn't just a future promise—a reward in the sky by and by. The kingdom of heaven is the place where God rules. So Jesus tells us that the influence of the kingdom is occurring right now. We don't always understand how all the pieces fit together, and the final blessings are not yet all in place, but trusting that God is working all things toward his perfect ends enables us to experience this promise now as well as in eternity.

An analogy might help this blessing make sense. Kathy and I were in an attorney's office recently making out our wills. We hope that we have no immediate need of them, but we are considering the future security of our children. We trust that there will be blessing for them down the road. But the reality is that if our children really needed anything from us now for their ultimate safety and security, we would say, "All that we have is yours already."

That's what God is saying to us. "My kingdom is yours for the future, but all that I have is already being applied to your spiritual well-being now." The Lord is working all things together so that his kingdom's rule and resources are already being applied to our eternal good.

God's third promise is this: "When you go through hard times, you're in good company." God assures us that every trial is not a consequence of his abandonment or our sin. Whenever we face abuse or harassment for our faith, Jesus reminds us, "So they persecuted the prophets who were before you" (Matt. 5:12).

We can imagine ourselves standing before the Lord in heaven and saying, "God, when I took a stand for you, my life got tough." He might reply, "Well, then, sit over there at the table with Jeremiah and Daniel and Stephen."

"But, Lord, it wasn't just tough. When I stood for you, people got so mad at me they wanted to get rid of me. And they began to lie about me." He might say to us, "Then you need to sit at the table with Joseph and Paul and Jesus. You're in good company. You're not strange or odd, and you're not alone."

When we are persecuted for taking a stand, we can be strengthened by the blessings of God, the promises of the kingdom, and the fact that we're in good company. These truths enable us to display joy and peace to the world as part of our witness to God's eternal faithfulness, even during our present hardship.

Being Salt and Light

We are blessed and kept for a reason. Jesus says to his followers, "You are the salt of the earth" (Matt. 5:13). Because a little bit of salt can go a long way, Jesus is saying, "You're on my mission with greater influence than you know. We're in this together. Even though the evil you are facing can seem overwhelming, a few grains of salt can have a significant effect in my Father's recipe that is designed to have others taste him."

Jesus gives an even more compelling image when he talks about Christians being the light of the world. I've been to the place where Jesus delivered his Sermon on the Mount. It's on a gently sloping hill above the Sea of Galilee. While I was there, I could imagine Jesus saying, "You are the light of the world. A city set on a hill cannot be hidden" (Matt. 5:14).

I could also envision what Jesus was pointing to. Around the Sea of Galilee are various hills, and the one that gets the most attention is known as the Arbel. On the top of the Arbel was a village, and at night people in a boat on the Sea of Galilee could look up and navigate by the light that shone from that village.

Another village named Capernaum was on the shore of the Sea of Galilee. Capernaum was the place where Jesus spent the most time in his public ministry, and it was a major intersection for land transportation in that portion of the Roman world. Those who needed to find that intersection could also navigate by the light on the hill.

Without too much imagination we can understand Jesus using the Arbel to assure his followers, "You have the ability to be a light for those on land or sea who need to know about me." Elsewhere Jesus tells us that he is the light of the world (John 8:12), but here he encourages us to shine his light for all.

In the early 1990s a delegation of evangelicals went to China to speak to the then president, Jiang Zemin, about relieving some of the political pressure on Christians in that nation. As the delegation met with him, someone asked, "Could we give you this Gospel of John from the Bible?"

After he agreed to accept it, he was then asked, "Would you be willing to read it?" His response was, "Yes, I'll read it, because when I was a little child, the nurse who took care of me was a Christian. I will read it for her sake."

Many months later, the pressure on Christians in China did begin to ease. And until recent government crackdowns, Christianity has flourished in China to a degree unknown since the earliest centuries of Christ's church.

I would not claim to know all the reasons why this flourishing has happened. But I do know that decades ago God said to a young Christian nurse in Jiang Zemin's household, "You can be salt and light to this boy." Her willingness to be a witness in her work may have been instrumental in changing the future of China and the course of Christianity's future worldwide.

God is still calling each of us to be salt and light in our workplace. Jesus urges us to be bold in our witness, saying, "Neither do people light a lamp and put it under a basket, but on a stand, and it gives light to the whole house" (Matt. 5:15). That verse reminds me of the children's song that says, "This little light of mine, I'm gonna let it shine." But the truth is not just for children.

When we shine Christ's truths and his character in our places of work, we are bringing his light to our (and our coworkers') world. How? We can ask a coworker in a time of grief, "Can I pray for you?" We can say to someone whose kids are struggling, "There's a youth group at our church. Maybe there are some kids there that your child could relate to."

Even when someone is complimenting you for your work, you can spread some spiritual salt and shine some gospel light by saying something like, "I'm just thankful the Lord brought me here so that

I could participate in what this company is doing." Our words do not have to sound like a sermon to be salt and light in the workplace.

Our Works Are as Important as Our Words

Jesus also tells us about how witness becomes effective, when he says, "Let your light shine before others, so that they may see your good works and give glory to your Father who is in heaven" (Matt. 5:16). Our works are as important as our words in providing witness to the character and love of our Savior.

Yes, our attitudes are important. And our words are important. But there's nothing more important than our works. If we quote Bible verses to people but have shoddy work or selfish habits, we can destroy our witness. The same is true if we're constantly late for work but excuse ourselves because we were "at a Bible study" or were "leading a prayer group."

Jesus helps us understand that all honest work is holy work. Whatever we do to glorify the Father places us on holy ground. We should not excuse ourselves from work responsibilities with the reasoning that our job is not as important as some optional spiritual activity. Work is worship. If we work with diligence and care, our jobs glorify God (1 Cor. 10:31; Col. 3:17). That means the quality and character of our work should display the character and care of our God. So good and responsible work is both witness and worship.

When we work with integrity, we reflect God's integrity and righteousness. When we work with care for our craft and care for those who work with us, we demonstrate God's care. When we consider the impact of the products we make on God's people and world, we honor God's creatures and creation.

The quality of our work should help to secure the livelihood of others as well as our own. In this way we apply our skills to the provision and protection of those precious to Jesus. We strive for excellence so that employees and customers can flourish according to God's intentions. In these ways and many more, we honor God through our work and daily offer witness to his grace.

When we employ the unique gifts God has given us, we're also celebrating his creativity. He has made each of us in his image with unique gifts, talents, and desires. All of these can become part of our witness in the workplace. The novelist Dorothy Sayers says it this way:

The Church's approach to an intelligent carpenter is usually confined to exhorting him not to be drunk and disorderly in his leisure hours, and to come to church on Sundays. What the Church *should* be telling him is this: that the very first demand that his religion makes upon him is that he should make good tables.

Church by all means, and decent forms of amusement, certainly—but what use is all that if in the very center of his life and occupation he is insulting God with bad carpentry? No crooked table legs or ill-fitting drawers ever, I dare swear, came out of the carpenter's shop at Nazareth. Nor, if they did, could anyone believe that they were made by the same hand that made Heaven and earth.

No piety in the worker will compensate for work that is not true to itself; for any work that is untrue to its own technique is a living lie.[2]

Jesus would have honed his carpentry work and in doing so would have honored his God. That's the opportunity God is giving us. The quality of our work should cause people to ask, "Why do you care so much about excellence in the workplace?" "Why are you so committed to integrity in your job?" "Why are you willing to go against the current of our culture when your ethics are on the line?" Such questions give us the opportunity to point to our God's character and the reasons we trust him. We can respond by saying, "The Lord let me work here. He gave me these talents. And I'm obligated to use them in ways that honor him." We also take such opportunities to point to the grace of God that's greater than our own talents and abilities.

In 1989, United Airlines flight 811 took off from Honolulu with 337 passengers and eighteen crew members onboard. At 22,000 feet the cargo door blew off. "The door swung out with such force that it passed its normal stop and slammed into the side of the fuselage, bursting the fuselage open. . . . The pilots initially believed that a bomb had gone off inside the airplane, as this accident happened just two months after Pan Am Flight 103 was blown up over Lockerbie, Scotland. They began an emergency descent in order to reach an altitude where the air was breathable, while also performing a 180-degree left turn to fly back to Honolulu."[3]

The pilot of the aircraft was David Cronin. He brought thirty-eight years of experience to the task of getting the people down safely. After the landing, he was asked by a reporter, "What did you do when the cargo door blew?" He replied, "I said a prayer for them [the passengers] momentarily, and got back to business."[4] That was his testimony. He knew that after praying for those onboard, his job was to land the plane safely.

Jesus calls us to give glory to the Father by the words and the work that we do.

It's all part of our calling.

It's not rocket science.

And it's not a terrible cross to bear.

When we do a good job, others will say, "I want to know about the God that helps you work this way! Tell me about him." Then tell them about the one to whom your work gives witness.

Notes

Chapter 1: Dignity

1. Cited in Amy L. Sherman, *Kingdom Calling* (Downers Grove, IL: InterVarsity Press, 2011), 232–33.
2. Cited in Sherman, *Kingdom Calling*, 232–33.
3. Gregory J. Roden, "Unborn Children as Constitutional Persons," National Library of Medicine, accessed December 3, 2021, https://www.ncbi.nlm.nih.gov/.
4. Daniel Victor, "Ethan Couch, 'Affluenza Teen' Who Killed 4 While Driving Drunk, Is Free," *New York Times*, April 2, 2018, https://nytimes.com.
5. N. Gregory Mankiw, "Why Aren't More Men Working?," *New York Times*, June 15, 2018, https://nytimes.com.
6. Cited in Scott Rae, "Made for Responsibility," in *The Pastor's Guide to Fruitful Work and Economic Wisdom: Understanding What Your People Do All Day*, ed. Drew Cleveland and Greg Forster (Overland Park, KS: Made to Flourish, 2012), 107n94.
7. Lester DeKoster, *Work: The Meaning of Your Life*, 2nd ed. (Grand Rapids, MI: Acton Institute, 2010), chap. 1.
8. Rosalind Cook, as summarized from "Permission for Passion," in Lloyd Reeb, *The Second Half* (Charlotte, NC: Lloyd Reeb & Halftime, 2012), 13–14.

Chapter 2: Purpose

1. *Sphere Sovereignty* (488), cited in *Abraham Kuyper, A Centennial Reader*, ed. James D. Bratt (Grand Rapids, MI: Eerdmans, 1998).
2. *It's a Wonderful Life*, directed by Frank Capra (New York: RKO Radio Pictures, 1946).

3. David Wright, "Made for Community" in *The Pastor's Guide to Fruitful Work and Economic Wisdom: Understanding What Your People Do All Day*, ed. Drew Cleveland and Greg Forster (Overland Park, KS: Made to Flourish, 2012), 92.

4. Personal letter from Casey and Rebekah Vance, December 2015.

Chapter 3: Integrity

1. Kenneth Bae, *Not Forgotten: The True Story of My Imprisonment in North Korea* (Nashville, TN: W Publishing, 2016), 155.

2. Bae, *Not Forgotten*, 156–57.

3. Kenneth Bae, "The Kenneth Bae Story: In His Own Words," trans. James Pearson, May 17, 2013, NK News, https://www.nknews.org.

4. *Cambridge English Dictionary*, s.v. "integrity," accessed December 3, 2021, https://dictionary.cambridge.org/.

5. Bae, *Not Forgotten*, 215–16.

6. Bae, *Not Forgotten*, 25.

7. Guilbert Gates, Jack Ewing, et al., "How Volkswagen's 'Defeat Devices' Worked," *New York Times*, updated March 16, 2017, https://nytimes.com.

8. "Gathering of Friends," pastors' colloquium, Atlanta, Georgia, circa 2013.

9. Bae, *Not Forgotten*, 171.

10. Michael Schrage, "Is VW's Fraud the End of Large-Scale Corporate Deception?," *Harvard Business Review*, September 29, 2015, https://hbr.org.

11. Bae, *Not Forgotten*, 155.

Chapter 4: Money

1. The Dirty Guv'nahs, "Under Control," track 8, *Hearts on Fire*, released March 11, 2014.

2. Steve Corbett and Brian Fikkert, *When Helping Hurts: How to Alleviate Poverty without Hurting the Poor . . . and Yourself* (Chicago: Moody, 2014).

3. Leo Sun, "A Foolish Take: Here's How Much Debt the Average U.S. Household Owes," *USA Today*, updated November 20, 2017, https://www.usatoday.com/.

Chapter 5: Success

1. Morgan Housel, "The World Loses a Great Investor," *USA Today*, February 28, 2014, https://www.usatoday.com/.

2. Timothy Keller, *Every Good Endeavor: Connecting Your Work to God's Work* (New York: Penguin, 2014), 221.

3. Julie Brown Patton, "Cam Newton Didn't Heed His Mom's Super Bowl 50 Text: 'Don't Let Devil Win Your Words,'" *Gospel Herald*, February 10, 2016, https://www.gospelherald.com/.

4. Horatius Bonar, "Not What These Hands Have Done," 1864.

Chapter 6: Humility

1. Jim Collins, "Good to Great: Fast Company," Jim Collins website, October 2001, https://www.jimcollins.com/.

2. Jim Collins, "The Misguided Mix-Up of Celebrity and Leadership," Conference Board Annual Report, Jim Collins website, September/October 2001, https://www.jimcollins.com/.

3. Megan Fowler, "Showing Up for the Suffering: A Conversation with Author Jill Buteyn, *By Faith*, Feb 15, 2016, http://byfaithonline.com/.

4. Jim Collins, "Hedgehog Concept," audio seminar, Jim Collins website, accessed January 5, 2022, https://www.jimcollins.com/.

5. "Famous Chef Accepts Christ, Finds True Joy," Sermon Illustrations, *Preaching Today*, February 2016, http://www.preachingtoday.com/.

Chapter 7: Glory

1. Lee Eclov, "Refreshing Hearts," *Preaching Today*, February 10, 2021, http://preachingtoday.com/.

2. Gerard Manley Hopkins, "The Principle or Foundation," in *Gerard Manley Hopkins: The Major Works*, ed. Catherine Phillips (New York: Oxford University Press, 2002), 292; emphasis added.

3. Martin Luther, adapted from "The Estate of Marriage," in Robert Alexander's *The Gospel-Centered Life at Work*, Leader's Guide (Greensboro, NC: New Growth Press, 2014), 13.

4. Dan Doriani, *Work: Its Purpose, Dignity, and Transformation* (Phillipsburg, NJ: P&R, 2019), 107–9.

5. Doriani, *Work*, 109–11.

6. Matthew Kaemingk and Cory B. Willson, *Work and Worship: Reconnecting Our Labor and Liturgy* (Grand Rapids, MI: Baker, 2020), 51.

7. Kaemingk and Willson, *Work and Worship*, 184.

8. Lesslie Newbigin, *Foolishness to the Greeks: The Gospel and Western Culture* (Grand Rapids, MI: Eerdmans, 1986), 143.

Chapter 8: Evil

1. Jimmy Dodd and Renaut Van Der Riet, *What Great Ministry Leaders Get Right* (Chicago: Moody, 2021), 54.
2. Cited in Matthew Kaemingk and Cory B. Willson, *Work and Worship: Reconnecting Our Labor and Liturgy* (Grand Rapids, MI: Baker, 2020), 43.
3. Kaemingk and Willson, *Work and Worship*, 45.
4. Stephen Smith, *Inside Job: Doing the Work within the Work* (Downers Grove, IL: InterVarsity Press, 2015), 22.
5. Cited in Nancy Guthrie, "Must We Be Hurt Deeply to be Used Significantly?," Crossway, Feb. 24, 2010, https://www.crossway.org/.
6. The leader, known to many of us, cited in Jerry Bridges, *The Discipline of Grace: God's Role and Our Role in the Pursuit of Holiness* (Colorado Springs: NavPress, 1994), 41.

Chapter 9: Leadership

1. Cal Thomas, "Dear God, Please Don't Let Me Be a Christian Leader," *Fundamentalist Journal* 3 (May 1984): 22–23.
2. William H. Willimon, "Why Leaders Are a Pain: Truth Telling in The Parish," *Christian Century*, February 8, 2016, https://www.christiancentury.org/.
3. Cited in Susan Fiske, "Wealth, Poverty, and Human Flourishing," *byFaith*, November 18, 2015, https://byfaithonline.com/.
4. Collin Hansen, "Revisiting 'Faithful Presence': 'To Change the World,' Five Years Later," The Gospel Coalition, November 12, 2015, https://www.thegospelcoalition.org/.

Chapter 10: Balance

1. "Jim Carrey's Search for Fulfillment," Sermon Illustrations, *Preaching Today*, accessed December 3, 2021, https://www.preachingtoday.com/.
2. Timothy Keller, *Every Good Endeavor: Connecting Your Work to God's Work* (New York: Penguin, 2014), 226–30.

Chapter 11: Witness

1. "Top 10 Most Challenged Books List," *Banned and Challenged Books*, accessed December 3, 2021, http://www.ala.org/.
2. Dorothy L. Sayers, *Letters to a Diminished Church: Passionate Arguments for the Relevance of Christian Doctrine* (Nashville, TN: Thomas Nelson, 2004), 139–40.

3. Wikipedia, s.v. "United Airlines Flight 811," updated October 27, 2021, https://en.wikipedia.org/.
4. Bruce Dunford, "Crew Relates Horror of United Flight 811," *AP News*, March 3, 1989, https://www.apnews.com/.

General Index

Scripture Index

Also Available from Bryan Chapell

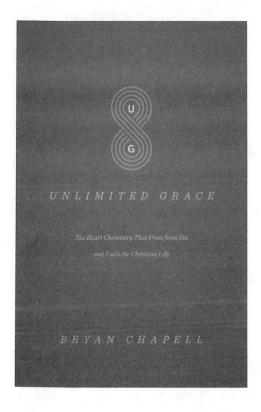

Unlimited Grace helps us to see how gospel joy transforms our hearts and makes us passionate for Christ's purposes. Bryan Chapell takes insights from a lifetime of relishing God's grace and pours them into this highly accessible and engaging book, helping readers see how God's grace shines through all of Scripture, for all of life.

For more information, visit **crossway.org**.